☼ *See Map F–B2* ★

C000050491

OLD TOWN HALL

Prague's Old Town Hall (*Staroměstská radnice*) dates back to 1338, but over the following 600 years it absorbed most of the buildings on the west side of Old Town Square. The grassland adjoining it indicates that part of

the building which was destroyed by the Nazis during the Prague Uprising in 1945. (The present Neo-Gothic **oriel tower** and **window** are reconstructions of the 14th-century originals.) Set into the pavement, 27 crosses commemorate the Protestant martyrs executed here after the Battle of the White Mountain in 1620. The **clock tower** was added in 1364 (its turrets added a century later) and its viewing gallery affords superb views over Prague. The tower wall bears a memorial plaque for the thousands of soldiers who died in the battle of liberation against the Nazis in 1944.

The hall's beautiful **astronomical clock** was constructed in the 1400s by **Master Hanuš**. It is surrounded by an intricate Gothic frame and 17th-century niche statuary. Stand in front of the clock on the hour to watch the ingenious mechanism at work.

The imposingly Gothic **entrance door** was built in the late 15th century and opens onto an entrance hall decorated with wall mosaics. Next to the door, ornate Renaissance windows incorporate Prague's historic coat of arms, which reads 'Prague, head of the Kingdom'.

Above: *A view from the tower of the Old Town Hall.*

<u>Old Town Hall</u>
✉ Staroměstské náměstí, Prague 1
☎ 224 228 456 or 236 002 562
🕓 Apr–Oct, Mon 11:00–18:00; Tue 09:00–18:00. Closes Nov–Mar at 17:00.
🚌 20-minute guided tour (book at Prague Information Service tourist office on the ground floor).
💰 Admission charge, plus an additional charge to climb the tower.
Ⓜ Staroměstská, Náměstí Republiky or Můstek (or tram: 5, 8, 14)

Above: *Sightseers enjoy walking across Charles Bridge.*

See Map G	★★★

CHARLES BRIDGE

Medieval Charles Bridge (*Karlův most*) is the city's most familiar landmark, affording spectacular views of Prague Castle and the river.

The view up to the castle is one of the most stunning in Prague, while along the river there are uninterrupted vistas. Southwards, you will see the Vltava's bridges, overlooked by Vyšehrad, while eastwards toward Old Town is a forest of spires and towers. Remember to return to the bridge at night – it's then that many buildings are illuminated and Prague takes on a romance and an atmosphere emphatically all its own.

Construction of the bridge began in 1357 at the command of Charles IV, to designs by his court architect **Peter Parler**. The Old Town side has the finer of the two gateways to the bridge, its tower decorated with its original Gothic carving and statuary: St Vitus with Charles IV on his right and Charles' son Václav IV on his left. The vacant western façade of the tower is the result of damage inflicted during the Thirty Years War – a battle in this war was fought here in 1648. There is a viewing gallery on the tower's first floor, and also access to the roof, both providing superb views of Prague Castle and the Lesser Quarter. The towers on the Lesser Quarter side are not as well preserved as the others, but the higher of the two can be climbed for a superb view of the bridge and its surroundings. The shorter tower was part of the earlier Judith Bridge swept away by the river.

Charles Bridge Statues

Most of the statues were put in place from 1683 to 1714, with the remainder added in the mid-19th century. Many have weathered badly and been removed. They are being replaced with modern copies. The statue of St John Nepomuk is the only bronze statue. The larger groupings of figures were among the first to be placed on the bridge: the Madonna and St Bernard are accompanied by symbols of Christ's Passion like the dice, the cock and the soldier's gauntlet; while the Madonna, St Dominic and St Thomas are shown with a dog, the emblem of the Dominicans. The large crucifix was for 200 years the only object on the bridge prior to the statues' arrival.

See Map B–D3   ★★★

CHURCH OF ST NICHOLAS

Dominating the Lesser Quarter Square (*see* page 26), the recently restored Church of St Nicholas (*sv. Mikuláš*) is without doubt the greatest Baroque church in Prague and the Dientzenhofers' supreme achievement.

Commissioned by the Jesuits, begun in 1703 and completed in 1761, it is a perfect example of the Baroque ambition to overwhelm the viewer and communicate an image of the infinite. Christoph, the older Dientzenhofer, was responsible for the general plan and façade, while son Kilian finished the dome and Anselmo Lurago added the belfry, the last part of the church to be built. The curving west façade, with its harmonious use of statuary, columns and pilasters, is deliberately understated so as to leave one unprepared for the drama of the interior. Imagine the effect such supremely confident architecture would have had on the poor Bohemian peasant of the time. The vast nave is covered in a similarly vast fresco by **Lukas Kracker** depicting the colourful exploits of St Nicholas (a.k.a. Santa Claus). The fabulous Baroque organ above the main door, was built in 1746, and was played by Mozart in 1787. The fresco above the organ shows St Cecilia, the patron saint of music. The enormous frescoed dome is 70m (230ft) high and celebrates the Holy Trinity. Statues of the Church Fathers point the way up to the high altar which is topped by a copper statue of St Nicholas.

Church of St Nicholas
✉ Malostranské náměstí 25, Malá Strana
☎ 257 534 215 (for concert information and tickets – concerts and organ recitals are held regularly, starting at 18:00.)
🕑 Open daily Apr–Oct, 09:00–17:00; Nov–Mar, 09:00–16:00;
climb the belfry, times as above.
🔔 Admission charge
M Malostranská
(or tram: 12, 22)

Below: *The amazing frescoed dome in the Church of St Nicholas.*

Wallenstein Palace
✉ Valdštejnské
náměstí 4, Prague
☎ 257 073 136
🕐 10:00–16:00 Sat
and Sun.
🚌 Free guided tour of
the Czech upper house
(within palace) 10:00–
16:00, Sat and Sun.
Ⓜ Malostranská
(or tram: 12, 18, 22)

Wallenstein Gardens
✉ Enter via palace's
main entrance.
🕐 10:00–18:00 daily
Apr–Oct, 09:00–19:00
daily May–Sep,
concerts sometimes
held in summer.
💰 Free

Art Gallery
✉ Riding Hall (palace's
former riding school)
🖥 www.ngprague.cz
🕐 10:00–18:00 Tue–Sun
💰 Admission charge,
depending on exhibi-
tions and concessions.

Below: *Statues line
a pathway in the
superb Wallenstein
Gardens.*

⭐ *See* Map B–E2   ★★★

WALLENSTEIN PALACE AND GARDENS

Wallenstein Palace (*Valdštejnský palác*), the first Baroque building of its type in Prague, was built for **Albrecht von Wallenstein**, military commander in the Thirty Years War. His ambition for the palace was to outdo Prague Castle, and he very nearly succeeded. Dozens of houses and gardens were purchased and then demolished in order for the palace to be constructed, work beginning in 1624 and ending six years later – most of it performed by Italian artists. The impressive interior has more grandeur than glory about it and probably reflects the cult of self which Wallenstein seems to have had, as he concerned himself with every last detail of the design.

The double-height main hall is the most memorable room, with a richly stuccoed ceiling framing a fresco which portray Wallenstein as a triumphant Mars riding his chariot. Used mainly for state functions, the hall occasionally hosts public concerts. After Mars, any last pretensions to humility are firmly laid to rest in the garden pavilion, where Wallenstein is depicted as Achilles lording it over gods and sundry heroic mortals.

The gardens are accessible only from Letenská. They include a series of 20th-century copies of statues by **Adriaen de Vries**, a grotto and ponds with fountains. The palace's riding school is used by the National Gallery for temporary exhibitions.

WALLENSTEIN PALACE & PRAGUE CASTLE

⚙ See Map C   ★★★

PRAGUE CASTLE

The castle (*Hrad*) has been the seat of power in Bohemia since the 9th century, although it has been rebuilt and added to many times since then. The official residence of presidents of the republic, it encloses St Vitus' Cathedral (*see* page 20) and is itself bordered by the ministries and agencies of government in Hradčany.

Less a castle and more a series of apartments, houses, palaces and churches, the castle's austere face gazes down upon the city. Its entrance is guarded by copies of the **fighting giants** sculpted by Ignaz Plazer. The human guards today are the presidential sentries, in their smart blue uniforms. At noon each day, the changing of the guard is accompanied by a brass band.

Further on, in the first courtyard, is the beautiful **Matthias Gate**. Originally a free-standing arch, it was later incorporated into a new façade, with the addition of staircases on each side which lead to the north and south wings of the castle. The south wing contains presidential apartments (not open to the public) while in the north wing is the Spanish Hall. This magnificent room, with its mirrors and chandeliers, is surely one of the most beautiful in Europe. Consult the concert listings – you may be lucky enough to see it.

The second courtyard is dominated by façades overlooked by the spires of St Vitus', while on the right is the little 18th-century Chapel of the Holy Cross, now an information and ticket office.

Above: *The royal coronation route ends at Prague Castle, guarded by dashing sentries.*

Prague Castle
✉ Hradčany
🖥 www.hrad.cz
🕐 Castle is open daily, 09:00–16:00,
☎ 224 373 368.
Other sights within the complex are open daily 09:00–17:00 Apr–Oct, 09:00–16:00 Nov–Mar. Picture gallery open daily 10:00–18:00, gardens open daily, 10:00–18:00.
Changing of the guard: on the hour 05:00–23:00 summer, 06:00–23:00 winter, fanfare at noon.
🚃 One-hour guided tours, audioguides.
♿ Most streets, courtyards and gardens can be entered freely. Various ticket options are available for the main sights and museums.
🍴 Reasonably priced cafés and restaurants.
Ⓜ Malostranská (or tram: 22, 23)

Above: *The spectacular twin spires and rose window that form part of the western facade of St Vitus' Cathedral.*

| See Map C | ★★★ |

ST VITUS' CATHEDRAL

The enormous Gothic pile of the cathedral (the largest in the Czech Republic) takes up most of the third courtyard of Prague Castle. The building owes its existence to Charles IV, who commissioned a French architect, Matthias of Arras, in the 1340s. Charles' later court architect **Peter Parler** took over and completed the eastern façade. Substantial work did not begin again until the 19th century and continued on and off until World War II. The oldest part of the exterior – the original Gothic of Parler – is to the east, while the western façade and spires are the more recent Neo-Gothic. The sheer scale of the interior is breathtaking, and much of the decoration is unashamedly exuberant. Peter Parler and Charles IV are depicted in the remarkably realistic Gothic sculptures that line the triforium in the inner choir.

All the 22 side chapels contain much to admire, but the **Tomb of St John Nepomuk** in the ambulatory will be enjoyed by all lovers of excess. The **Golden Gate** along from the tomb was for many centuries the main entrance to the cathedral. Parler's **Chapel of St Wenceslas** (*sv. Václav*) is a dazzling spectacle, and a door within the chapel leads to a chamber containing the Bohemian crown jewels (not normally accessible to the public). Opposite St Wenceslas Chapel is the **Habsburg Mausoleum** and the royal crypt, where lie the remains of some of the kings and queens of Bohemia.

St Vitus' Cathedral
✉ Prague Castle
(see page 19)
🕐 09:00–17:00 daily
Apr–Oct, 09:00–16:00
daily Nov–Mar
💰 Tower: admission
charge. Free entry into
main nave and St
Wenceslas Chapel. You
may enter the chancel or
crypt with a castle ticket.
All services are free.

St Vitus' Cathedral & Castle Square

See Map C–A2 ★★★

CASTLE SQUARE

Castle Square (*Hradčanské náměstí*) is just outside the main gates to the castle. Its grand palaces were built for the Catholic nobility in the early 17th century and are the result of reconstruction after the great fire of 1541 swept through the area.

The **Archbishop's Palace** (*Arcibiskupský palác*) proudly displays an extravagant Rococo façade which dates from the 1760s but incorporates a portal from an earlier period. The palace has been the seat of the Catholic archbishops of Prague since 1621. Opposite is the early 19th-century façade of the **Salm Palace** (*Salmovský palác*). Panoramic views of the city can be had from the area between the Salm Palace and the castle entrance.

A passage next to the Archbishop's Palace leads to Prague's **National Gallery European Art Collection** in the **Sternberg Palace** (*Sternberský palác*). The 18th-century palace is built around a central courtyard, while the art collection spans painting and sculpture from their beginnings to the 20th century (*see page 36*).

On the western side of Castle Square, the Czech Republic's foreign ministry is housed in the Baroque **Toscana Palace** (*Toskánský palác*), a monumental building completed in 1691. Its rather haughty appearance is softened by the delightful **Martinic Palace** (*Martinický palác*) to its right.

The Schwarzenberg Palace
Next door to the Salm Palace, *Schwarzenberský palác* is a superbly sgraffitoed building dating from 1563. The black and white design of the glorious façade deceives the eye into perceiving carved stone blocks, an effect which has made it one of Prague's most famous exteriors. Formerly home to the Military Museum, the interior is currently being renovated and will re-open in 2007 for exhibitions and cultural events.

Below: *Castle Square is lined with impressive palaces and mansions such as the Archbishop's Palace, which dates from the middle of the 18th century.*

⚜ *See* Map B–A3 ★★★

Strahov Monastery
✉ Královská Kanonie
Premonstrátů na
Strahové, Strahovské
nádvoří 1
☎ 220 516 6571
💻 www.
strahovmonastery.cz
🕐 09:00–18:00
Mon–Sat; Sun
10:00–18:00
💰 Admission charge
M Malostranská
(or tram: 22, 23)

Libraries
🕐 Daily 09:00–12:00,
13:00–17:00
💰 Admission charge

🍴 Oživle drevo
(Revived Wood)
☎ 220 517 274
💻 www.ozivledrevo.cz

🍴 Monastic
Restaurant / Brewery
☎ 233 356 552

STRAHOV MONASTERY

Now once more a working monastery and museum, *Strahovský klášter* was founded in 1140. It functioned during the closure of monasteries in 1783 by claiming exemption as an educational establishment – a fair claim, since it had amassed Bohemia's greatest library. That same library is now 800 years old and kept in the monastery's halls.

The **Philosophical Hall** (*Filosofický sál*) was built in 1782 to house an influx of books from a dissolved monastery in Moravia. It is a splendidly welcoming room, full of the walnut patina of its bookcases and the bindings of the books themselves. The fresco on the barrel-vaulted ceiling is by **Franz Maulbertsch** and is entitled *The Struggle of Mankind to Know Real Wisdom*. The **Theological Hall** (*Teologický sál*) is more intimate and possesses stucco-framed frescoes by one of the monks, plus some interesting 17th-century astronomical globes.

The church is a highly decorated Baroque affair, its outer façade having been designed by **Anselmo Lurago** in the 1750s. The interior is light and airy, its unusual ceiling painted with scenes from the life of St Norbert, founder of the Premonstratensian Order.

Strahov's **Museum of Czech Literature** (*Památník národního písemnictví*) and also its **Gallery** (*Strahovská obrazárna*) are excellent, but probably only of interest to aficionados. The monastery garden can be explored for great views over the city and connects with the adjoining Petřín Hill (*see* page 43).

See Map F–A2 ★★★

OLD-NEW SYNAGOGUE

This synagogue (*Staronová synagóga*) on Pařižská, in the Jewish Quarter, is the oldest functioning synagogue in Europe – building commenced in the 1270s – and the most important Jewish centre in Prague. Easily recognized by its distinctive 14th-century stepped-brick gable, it was originally called simply the New Synagogue, but became known as the Old-New after another synagogue was built nearby (it was later destroyed).

Above: *The distinctive gable of the historic Old-New Synagogue.*
Opposite: *The twin spires of Strahov Monastery look out across the city from Petřín Hill.*

You can go inside the synagogue by buying a ticket from the ticket office opposite the synagogue entrance. The main hall of the interior is bounded in part by **women's galleries**, which were added in the 18th century to allow them a view of proceedings. The doorway to the hall has a beautiful **tympanum** of carved grape clusters and vine leaves: the 12 bunches of grapes represent the 12 tribes of Israel. The rib-vaulted **main hall** contains the **Ark** – a shrine which holds the sacred scrolls of the Torah (the first five books of the Jewish Bible). This, the holiest place in the synagogue, is surrounded by candles and topped with a lovely 13th-century tympanum carved with leaves. Next to it is the **chair of the Chief Rabbi**, indicated by a small Star of David on the wall above. **Rabbi Löw**, a leading 16th-century scholar of the Talmud, used to sit here.

> **Old-New Synagogue**
> ✉ Červená 2, Josefov, (corner of Pařižská and Červená)
> ☎ 222 317 191
> ⊕ Apr–Oct daily 09:00–18:00; Nov–Mar daily 09:00–16:30
> 🎟 Admission charge, buy tickets at the Jewish Museum bookshop in the Jewish Town Hall, opposite the synagogue.
> M Staroměstská

⊙ *See* Map D–B1 | ★★★

Above: *The ornate staircase of the Troja Summer Palace is lined with mythical statuary.*

TROJA SUMMER PALACE

North of the city, on the banks of the Vltava River and within Troja Park, is the impressive red and white **Troja Summer Palace** (*Trojský zámek*), built in the late 17th century by **Jean-Baptiste Mathey** for the aristocratic Sternberg family. This delightful building, which is surely one of the most harmonious in Prague, sits amid formal French-style gardens (also designed by Mathey) with a water fountain, maze, open-air theatre and two orangeries – behind the palace there are vine-clad terraced hills. The exterior of the palace is based on a Classical Italian model with two projecting wings and turreted belvederes. The most prominent feature is the magnificent double staircase that climbs to the front door, its balustrading bristling with statues of gods and titans.

The sumptuously decorated interior of the palace took two decades to complete. The grand hall is one vast fresco depicting the glories of the Habsburg dynasty and the loyalty of the Sternberg family: Leopold I (1657–1705) is shown victorious over the Turks, his victims falling from the ceiling in the best traditions of trompe l'oeil. There are also smaller chambers with murals of Chinese landscapes.

Troja Summer Palace
⊠ U trojského zámku 1
☎ 283 851 614,
🖥 www.citygalleryprague.cz
📧 lectghmp@volny.cz
🕐 Apr–Oct 10:00–18:00, Tue–Sun; Nov–Mar 10:00–17:00, Sat and Sun
🚌 Guided tours are available.
💰 Admission charge
Ⓜ Nádraží Holešovice, then bus 112.

Troja Summer Palace & Clementinum

See Map F–A2 ★★

KLEMENTINUM

This former Jesuit college is the largest complex of Baroque buildings in Prague. The Jesuits were invited to the city by Ferdinand I in 1556 in order to win back converts from the heresy of the Hussites. Establishing themselves in the church and monastery of St Clement, they were soon able to rival and then surpass the city's Carolinum (Hussite college), eventually gaining complete control over Prague's higher education system in 1622. In 1773, the Order was dissolved by the pope and the Jesuits had to leave Prague, whereupon all education was put under state control.

There are five imposing courtyards, the first of which contains the entrance to the **Mirrored Chapel** (*Zrcadlová kaple*), all gilt and mirror panels. The excellent acoustics are the reason why so many concerts are held here (the chapel is otherwise seldom open). The **Baroque Hall**, near the chapel, is one of the loveliest rooms in Prague, decorated with beautiful frescoes and ancient globes. The leather-bound books are part of the vast collection of the **National Library**. This, and the **Observatory**, is accessible by guided tour. It was in the Observatory that Johannes Kepler studied the heavens on a daily basis in the early 1600s when he was court astronomer. Inside are charts, models of the solar system and other valuable astronomical paraphernalia but the big draw for tourists is the unsurpassable panoramic views of the city.

Klementinum
⊠ Karlova 1 (second entrance on Mariánské náměstí)
☎ 603 231 241
🕓 14:00–18:00 Mon–Fri; Sat, Sun 11:00–18:00
🚊 Tours of the Library and Observatory (a.k.a. Astronomical Tower) on the hour.
🎫 Tickets sold in advance, maximum 25 per group.
Ⓜ Staroměstská (or tram 17, 18)

National Library
⊠ Mariánské náměstí 4, Prague 1, Staré Město
☎ 221 666 311
💻 www.nkp.cz
🕓 09:00–19:00 Mon–Sat
Ⓜ Staroměstská

Below: *The Baroque buildings of the Clementinum, a former Jesuit college.*

⊙ *See* Map B–E2 | ★★

Liechtenstein Palace
On the west side of the square, *Lichtenštejnský palác* is a combination of five houses whose classical façade was added in the 1790s. It was home to Karl von Liechtenstein, who pronounced the death sentence on the 27 martyrs executed in Old Town Square. The palace holds concerts and art exhibitions.
✉ Malostranské náměstí 13
☎ P.I.S. 257 534 206

Kaiserstein Palace
✉ Malostranské náměstí 23

Concerts:
☎ 224 224 351
🖥 www.opera-rkm.cz
✆ info@opera-rkm.cz

🍽 **U Mecenáše**
Ancient and elegant restaurant; serves good game dishes.
✉ Malostranské náměstí 10, Prague 1
☎ 257 531 631
🕐 17:00–24:00 Mon–Fri, 12:00–24:00 Sat and Sun

LESSER QUARTER SQUARE

Charles Bridge leads to the bustling Lesser Quarter Square (*Malostranské náměstí*), which was created in the mid-13th century. Principally a large marketplace, it had its own pillory and gallows. Medieval structures are concealed behind Renaissance and Baroque façades, and many houses have been knocked together to form palaces. In the medieval arcades around the square, you will find shops and cafés.

The square is dominated and divided in two by the magnificent **Church of St Nicholas** (*see* page 17). On the east side of the square at no. 23, the **Kaiserstein Palace** (*Kaiserštejnský palác*) has a detailed Baroque façade with four gable statues personifying the seasons. Number 21 is the former **Lesser Quarter Town Hall** (*Malostranské radnice*), with a Renaissance façade incorporating a distinctive main portal. The **Sternberg Palace** (*Sternberský palác*) at no. 19 on the north side is built where the great fire of 1541 began. Number 18, next door, is the twin-turreted **Smiřický Palace** (*Palác Smiřických*). This green and yellow extravaganza was where the Second Defenestration of Prague (*see* page 8) was plotted. Sněmovní, the road off the square in front of the Smiřický Palace, is the home of the Czech National Assembly.

The south side of the square contains vestiges of medieval Prague, with the 16th-century **Golden Lion House** (*U Mecenáše*) at no. 10 retaining its 13th-century cellar.

See Map C–C2 ★★

Left: *The Baroque exterior of the Basilica of St George.*
Opposite: *Tram 22 stops in Lesser Quarter Square.*

BASILICA AND CONVENT OF ST GEORGE

Adjacent to the Old Royal Palace (*see* page 35) is the Basilica of St George (*sv. Jiří*). Despite its red Baroque façade, its fabric is restored Romanesque. Founded in 921 by Prince Vratislav, the basilica and adjoining convent were rebuilt in 1142 after a fire.

The typically stark Romanesque interior has excellent acoustics and there are occasional concerts held here, with the Baroque chancel staircase used as a stage for the musicians. The most notable features inside are the **tombs of St Ludmilla and Vratislav** – the latter a simple wooden casket.

The **Convent of St George** (*Klášter sv. Jiří*) was the first such institution in Bohemia. Its first abbess was Mlada, great-granddaughter of St Ludmilla and sister to Prince Boleslav II. In 1782 the convent was abolished and the building turned into barracks and storerooms, but in 1974 it was taken over by the National Gallery (*see* panel, page 38).

Basilica of St George
⊠ St George's Square (*Jiřské náměstí*) 33, Pražský hrad
☎ 257 320 536
🕘 09:00–17:00 daily Apr–Oct, 09:00–16:00 daily Nov–Mar
🜔 Admission with Prague Castle ticket (*see* page 19).
Ⓜ Malostranská or Hradčanská

Convent of St George (National Gallery)
⊠ Next to the basilica
🖥 www.ngprague.cz
📧 web@ngprague.cz
🕘 10:00–18:00 Tue–Sun
🜔 Admission charge
Ⓜ Malostranská or Hradčanská

See Map F–B2 ★★

JOSEFOV

Josefov – the Jewish Quarter – contains some beautiful and haunting traces of the historic community which lived and worked here. For centuries, the Jews of Prague had to endure the prejudice and oppression of their Christian neighbours. Enclosed in their own ghetto and subject to restrictive laws, it was not until 1784 and the reforms of Joseph II (after whom the Jewish Quarter was named) that some degree of freedom was attained. What remains of Josefov today survived the slum clearance project of the 1890s, when most of the area – which lacked all sanitation – was razed and replaced by Art-Nouveau mansions for the wealthy.

Like the Jews throughout Europe, the Prague Jews suffered appallingly under the Nazis. During the German occupation of Prague, Jewish people were transported to the purpose-built ghetto of Terezín and thence to extermination camps: some 36,000 were to die there. The historic synagogues and cemetery of Josefov survive today only because of Hitler's ghoulish plan to preserve Prague's old ghetto as a museum of an extinct race. There is still a small Jewish community in Prague and some synagogues remain places of worship.

Pařížská ulice heads north from Old Town Square practically dividing Josefov in half. Its shops and restaurants inhabit buildings erected in the 1890s with many fine examples of Art-Nouveau architecture along its length.

Josefov Town Hall
(*Zidovská radnice*)
Had a Baroque facelift in 1763 but its core structure is from 1570.
✉ Opposite Old–New Synagogue.

Old-New Synagogue
(*Staronová synagóga*)
See page 23

High Synagogue
(*Vysoká synagóga*)
Once part of the town hall. ✉ Adjacent to the town hall, on Červená.

Maisel Synagogue
(*Maiselova synagóga*)
Contains an exhibition relating to Prague Jewry.
✉ Maiselova

Spanish Synagogue
(*Spanělská synagóga*)
Moorish exterior, ornate interior. ✉ Vězeňská

Pinkas Synagogue
(*Pinkasova synagóga*)
Memorial interior with lists of Holocaust victims.
✉ Siřoká
🎫 Tickets for all sights from U Staré školy 1,
☎ 224 819 456

See Map F–C2 ★★

MUNICIPAL HOUSE

Linked by an arch to the Powder Gate at the Celetná entrance to Old Town, the splendid Municipal House (*Obecní dům*) stands on the site of King Vladislav Jagiello's 15th-century royal court and is undoubtedly Prague's best Art-Nouveau building.

Completed in 1911 as an arts and cultural centre, the building was designed by **Osvald Polívka** and **Antonín Balšánek**. The domed façade has a large semicircular mosaic entitled *Tribute to Prague* and is richly decorated with stucco and statuary. But it is the inside of the building that is particularly worth seeing, for virtually every fitment in every room is original: if you dine in one of the cafés and restaurants you'll be able to view everything in comfort. You may also be able to join a guided tour to view some of the outstanding sculptural detailing of **Alfons Mucha**, plus the paintings and mosaics of the greatest Czech artists of the day. The **Smetana Hall** is the city's largest concert venue (*see page 74*).

Municipal House
✉ náměstí Republiky 5, Prague 1
♿ Free to restaurants, cafés, bars and shop.
🍴 American Bar, Francouzská restaurace, Plzeňská restaurace
Ⓜ Náměstí Republiky (or tram: 5, 8, 14)

Municipal House Information Centre
Sells tickets for a tour of the main rooms of Municipal House (♿ admission charge) and concerts in Smetana Hall. Times vary, book ahead.
✉ Ground floor, Municipal House.
☎ 222 002 101
📠 222 002 100
🖥 www.obecnidum.cz
🖱 info@obecnidum.cz
🕐 10:00–18:00

Municipal House Coffee Shop
✉ Municipal House
☎ 222 002 763
📠 222 002 761
🖱 kavarna.od@vysehrad2000.cz
🕐 07:30–23:00 Mon–Sun

Opposite: *A detail of the Town Hall in Prague's Jewish Quarter.*
Left: *Part of the Municipal House complex, the impressive Smetana Hall is Prague's largest concert venue.*

☼ See Map I   ★★

VYŠEHRAD

Vyšehrad (literally 'castle on the heights') is a rocky eminence next to the southern boundary of New Town. It overlooks the Vltava and has a superb view along the river to the cathedral, which is about 3km (2 miles) away.

The remains of Vyšehrad fortress are set in a peaceful landscaped park at the summit of the hill. The walls and ramparts can be wandered around at leisure: the western entrance to the fortress is the 17th-century **Tábor Gate**, adjacent to which are the remains of Charles IV's 14th-century fortifications. Two further gates are the original Gothic **Špička Gate** and the 17th-century **Leopold Gate**.

The Romanesque **Rotunda of St Martin** (sv. Martina) – heavily restored in the 19th century – is the only remnant of the original medieval fortress. The western side of the fortress is more spectacular: the hill turns abruptly into a steep cliff above the Vltava, and the remains of the fortress cling to the side of the hill. There are great views here and you can also peer into **Libuše's Baths**. Within the fortress area there is a small museum and a permanent exhibition in a Neo-Gothic deanery.

On the northwest slopes is the **Church of St Peter and St Paul** (sv. Petr a Pavel), built in the 1880s on the site of an 11th-century basilica – remains of the earlier structure are visible in the church. The twin spires of this Neo-Gothic edifice were added in the early 1900s.

Vyšehrad Fortress
✉ Soběslavova 1, Vyšehrad
☎ 241 410 348
🖥 www. praha-vysehrad.cz
✆ vysehrad@ zris.mepnet.cz
🍴 Wine bar (vinárna) opposite church of St Peter and St Paul, café near information centre, and pubs in streets below fortress.
Ⓜ Vyšehrad (or tram: 7, 8 or 24 to Albertov)

Information Centre
✉ Špička Gate, V Pevnosti St, Vyšehrad fortress
🕐 09:30–17:30 daily

Church of St Peter and St Paul
✉ Vyšehrad fortress
🕐 09:30–17:30

Vyšehrad Gallery
✉ Above Libuše's Baths.
🕐 09:30–17:00 daily

VYŠEHRAD & TÝN CHURCH

See Map F–B2 ★

TÝN CHURCH

Týn Church (*Matka boží před Týnem*) is an inspiring 14th-century Gothic edifice whose twin towers and 18 spires dominate **Old Town Square** (*see* page 14) and are a Prague landmark. Visible from all over the city, it is actually impossible to gain an unobstructed view of the church due to the houses built right up against it. Until their defeat, the Hussites claimed the church as

their own, but after their overthrow in 1432 the church reverted to Catholicism, and the gold statue of the Madonna on the gable was formed from the melted-down communion chalice of the Hussite king George of Poděbrad.

A narrow alley off the arcade next to the House of the Stone Bell on Old Town Square leads to the front of the church, but to see the splendid entrance doorway on the north side of the church you'll have to circle round past the rear of the building via Celetná. The door was constructed in 1390 and depicts scenes from Christ's Passion. The chief attraction in the Baroque and Neo-Gothic interior is the marble tomb of court astronomer **Tycho Brahe**, but the 15th-century pulpit is equally interesting.

Above: *Dominating Old Town Square is Gothic Týn Church.*
Opposite: *The twin spires of The Church of St Peter and St Paul can be seen from everywhere on Vyšehrad.*

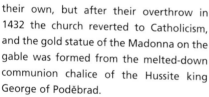

Týn Church
⊠ Old Town Square (*Staroměstské náměstí 14*), Staré Město,
☎ 222 318 186
🖳 www.tynska.fa.mosk.cz
🕘 Mass only. 16:30 Mon–Fri, 13:00 Sat; 21:00 Sun
💰 Free

Above: *Some interesting Baroque buildings line Nerudova Street.*

See Map B–C2 | ★

NERUDOVA STREET

Nerudova Street (*Nerudova ulice*) heads upwards toward the castle from the northwest corner of Lesser Quarter Square. It's a steep, narrow road and quite a climb, although the panoramic views at the top are well worth the effort. Historically, this is where the city's artists made their home and you will still see craft shops and galleries dotted around, although they are outnumbered these days by cafés and beer halls. The street is named after the writer **Jan Neruda**, who lived in the **House at the Two Suns** (no. 47) in the middle of the 19th century. The house has its own sign with said suns, just one of many similarly interesting signs along Nerudova. Look out for the **Red Eagle** (no. 6), the **Three Fiddles** (no. 12), the **Golden Cup** (no. 16), the **Golden Key** (no. 27), the **Golden Horseshoe** (no. 34), the **Red Lion** (no. 41), the **Green Lobster** (no. 43) and the **White Swan** (no. 49).

The **Morzin Palace** (*Morzinský palác*) at number 5 is the Romanian embassy. The façade includes a first-floor balcony supported by two beefy Moors (a pun on 'Morzin') sculpted by **Ferdinand Brokof**. The sculptures are so large that they take over the pavement. The **Thun-Hohenstein Palace** (*Thun-Hohenštejnský palác*) at number 20 – the Italian embassy – can be identified easily by its two eagles sculpted by **Matthias Braun**.

See Map F–C4 | ★

WENCESLAS SQUARE

Prague's most famous square is the hub of New Town (*Nové Město*), and is less a square than a long, tree-lined boulevard. Wenceslas Square (*Václavské náměstí*) is a bustling, vibrant place of hotels, discos, clubs and stores. In medieval times it was a horse market, but there is no sign of that now – the square's oldest building is from the 18th century, while the rest were built predominantly over the last 100 years.

The **Koruna Palace** (*palác Koruna*) at the northern end was built in 1914, while the **Peterkův dům** (no. 12) dates from the 1890s and was one of Prague's first Art-Nouveau buildings. It was designed by **Jan Kotěra**, while the **Hotel Juliš** (no. 22) was designed by **Pavel Janák**. Almost opposite the hotel is the **Assicurazioni Generali** building. This modern study in Baroque (now the Polish Cultural Institute) was the insurance office in which **Franz Kafka** worked in 1906–7.

The **Wiehl House**, on the opposite corner, was built in 1896 by **Antonín Wiehl** and is recognizable by its Art-Nouveau sgraffito and trompe l'oeil friezes. Next door is **Melantrich House** where Hável and Dubček appeared to the crowds during the Velvet Revolution. Nearby is the **Lucerna Palace**, a vast Moorish shopping arcade designed in the early 1900s. Discover the charm of an earlier era by stopping for a drink at the **Hotel Evropa**, opposite the Lucerna. The lavishly ornate Art-Nouveau exterior is matched by an equally exuberant interior.

Wenceslas Monument

In the middle of the southern end of the square, in front of the National Museum, is the statue of St Wenceslas (*see* also panel, page 8). A statue of the saint has stood in the square since the late 1600s, though the present monument was placed here in 1912. Cast in bronze, the huge figure of Wenceslas astride his steed is surrounded by the statues of various other Czech saints. The monument is one of the city's focal points for protest and oratory. An unofficial Memorial to the Victims of Communism (*Obětem komunismu*) sits in front of the monument: the wreaths, photographs and crosses are simple and eloquent.

Below: Wenceslas Square as seen from Wenceslas Monument.

Above: *The splendid Baroque interior of the Church of St James.*

Vinohrady Churches
The **Church of the Sacred Heart** (*Nejsvětější Srdce Páně*) on náměstí Jiřího z Poděbrad was built in 1928 by Josip Plečník: its giant clock face and mixture of styles win it much admiration. Nearby on U vodárny is Pavel Janák's 1930s **Hussite Church** (*Husův sbor*): the chalice on its tower is a symbol of the Hussite faith; the plaque commemorates the church's part in the 1945 Prague Uprising. Josef Gočár's interwar **Church of St Wenceslas** (*sv. Václav*) on náměstí Svatopluka Cecha has a dramatically stepped roof and pencil tower.

Churches
St Nicholas

Facing the Old Town Hall, *sv. Mikuláš* was built in the 1730s and designed by Kilian Ignaz Dientzenhofer. Its glorious Baroque façade fronts an intimate interior with a magnificent dome and chandelier. Concerts are often held here.
⊠ *Old Town Square,*
M *Staroměstská,*
⊕ *daily, 09:00–16:00 Nov–Mar 10:00–17:00 (Sat, Sun).*

St James

This Gothic church (*sv. Jakub*) was founded in 1232 and was remodelled in Baroque style in the late 17th century. It has a splendid Baroque organ, more than 20 side chapels and a beautiful Baroque tomb of Count Vratislav of Mitrovice.
⊠ *Mala Štupartská,*
☎ *224 828 816,*
M *Náměstí Republiky,*
⊕ *09:30–12:15, 14:00–16:00 Mon–Sat, 08:00, 09:00, 10:30 Sun,*
♦ *free.*

St Francis

This domed church (*sv. František*) was the official church of the Knights of the Cross with the Red Star. It is the only one of its kind in the city – designed by Jean-Baptiste Mathey, it follows a French rather than Italian interpretation of Baroque. It has a magnificent altar and striking statues of saints. Next door is the medieval crypt and an exhibition of religious art and treasures.
⊠ *Knights of the Cross Square (Křižovnické náměstí), Staré Město.*
⊕ *Exhibition open May–Oct, Tue–Sun, 10:00–13:00, 14:00–18:00; Nov–Apr 10:00–13:00, 14:00–17:00*

St Thomas

Sv. Tomáše was originally a Gothic church finished in 1379, but was remodelled by Kilian Ignaz Dientzenhofer in 1723. He preserved the Gothic ground-plan and spire, added a dome and created a new Baroque façade. Inside are Václav Reiner's trompe l'oeil ceiling frescoes.

✉ *Josephská 8, (off Letenská), Malá Strana,* **M** *Malostranská, (tram: 12, 22),* ⏰ *10:30–13:00, 14:30–18:00,* 💰 *free.*

St Ignatius

Sv. Ignác, one of Prague's most elaborate Baroque churches, was built by the Jesuits during the Counter-Reformation. The curlicued exterior features statues of St Ignatius of Loyola – the founder of the Jesuits – while the interior is a riot of stucco and gilt ornamentation.

✉ *Nové Město,* ☎ *224 921 254*

Historic Buildings

Goltz-Kinský Palace

On the east side of Old Town Square is the decorative red stonework of the *Palác Golz-Kinských*, designed by Dientzenhofer. In the 19th century Kafka's father owned a shop here. Today it houses the National Gallery's graphic collection. The adjoining Stone Bell House is used for exhibitions and concerts.

✉ *Staroměstské náměstí 12, Staré Město,* ☎ *224 810 758,* 🖳 *www.ngprague.cz* ⏰ *10:00–18:00 Tue–Sun,* 💰 *50Kč.*

Old Royal Palace

Starý Královský palác was home to the monarchs of Bohemia for 600 years until the 16th century, when it became an administrative headquarters and the Bohemian parliament. The cellars (*see* panel) comprise the remnants of the Romanesque palace of 1135. The Přemyslids and Charles IV built on top of this and it was finished off with the 15th-century Vladislav Hall. The parliament was destroyed by the fire of 1541 and rebuilt 20 years later.

Castle History

The Gothic cellars are now home to a fascinating new exhibition: The Story of Prague Castle. Encompassing more than 5000 years of history it features more than 500 exhibits, 90% of them original, including the Funeral Crown of Rudolph of Hapsburg and a magnificent coronation sword. The site also contains models, videos and documentaries, while visitors get to see parts of the castle previously accessible only to staff, including the Tower of Wenceslas IV and the Charles IV Arcade.

⏰ Open daily 09:00–17:00 (bring a coat or sweater as the average temperature is a chilly 8°C).
💰 Admission charge

Below: *The ornate organ in the Church of St Thomas.*

Old Bohemian Art Collection, Convent of St Agnes

The collection – arranged in chronological order – covers the 14th–17th centuries, starting in the crypt with 14th-century Czech art. Most of these works are typical of the period: deeply symbolic, devotional and originally intended for church altars. Moving to the later Gothic on the ground floor, one can trace the development of such art from its initial abstractions to an increased realism. There are also many examples of Gothic woodcarving and sculpture.

✉ U Milosrdných 17, Anezská 1
☎ 221 879 111
🕓 10:00–18:00 Tue–Sun
💰 Admission charge.

Below: *The Singing Fountain in the Belvedere's gardens emits a merry tinkle.*

✉ *third courtyard, Prague Castle.*

The Belvedere

One of the best examples of Renaissance architecture in northern Europe. Built for Anne, wife of Ferdinand I, and designed by the Genoese Paolo della Stella, construction began in 1538 and was completed in 1564. It is a wonderfully harmonious building with a graceful Ionic colonnade, and the copper-clad roof is shaped like an inverted ship's hull. It now hosts art exhibitions.

✉ *Prague Castle,*
🕓 *10:00–18:00 Tue–Sun (only during exhibitions).*

Museums and Galleries
Museum of Fine Arts

The museum inhabits the House of the Black Madonna (*Dům U Černé Matky boží*), itself built in 1911 by Cubist architect **Josef Gočár**. The Black

Madonna is on the first floor. The museum has a permanent exhibition devoted to Cubism, plus space for temporary exhibitions.

✉ *Ovocný trh 19, Staré Město,* ☎ *224 211 746,* 🕓 *10:00– 18:00 Tue–Sun,*
💰 *admission charge*

Picture Gallery

Prague Castle's royal stables were renovated in the mid-1960s and now house the castle's art collection (*Obrazárna Pražského hradu*). Emperor Rudolf II's collection was plundered by the Swedes in 1648, and the National Gallery has most of the rest, but what remains here is well worth seeing. Most artworks were produced in the 16th to 18th centuries.

✉ *former stables, second courtyard, Prague Castle,*
🕓 *10:00–18:00,*
💰 *admission charge*

National Gallery European Art Collection

The **Italian art**

collection from 1300 to 1500 comprises glorious Gothic panel paintings. There is a fine selection of beautiful Eastern European and Byzantine icons, plus canvases by the Flemish artists **Breughel the Younger** and **Breughel the Elder**. The collection of German, Flemish and Dutch art covers the period from around 1350–1700. There are also works by Albrecht Dürer, Lucas Cranach, Rubens and Rembrandt.

⊠ *Sternberg Palace, Hradčanské náměstí 15 Hradčany (tram: 22, 23),* ☎ *220 514 634,* ⌨ *www.ngprague.cz* ⏰ *10:00–18:00 Tue–Sun,* 🛈 *admission charge.*

National Gallery of Modern Art

The *Galerie moderního umění* inhabits the Trade Fairs Building, completed in 1928. The collection includes 20th-century Czech art and 19th- and 20th-century French paintings by Impressionists, post-Impressionists and Cubists, as well as other modern masterpieces. The Czech collection includes works by Surrealists Jindřich Štyrský, Marie Čermínová and Vincenc Makovsky.

⊠ *Trade Fair Palace (Veletržní palác), Dukelských hrdinů 47, Holešovice,* ☎ *224 301 003,* ⌨ *www. ngprague.cz* ⏰ *10:00–18:00 Tue–Wed, Fri–Sun, 10:00–21:00 Thu,* 🛈 *200Kč (3 floors), 150Kč (2 floors),* 🎧 *audiotour included,* Ⓜ *Nádraží Holešovice, then tram 5, 12, 17.* 🛈 *admission charge.*

Decorative Arts Museum (UPM)

Within the Jewish Quarter, in a 19th-century Neo-Renaissance building, the UPM (*Umělecko-průmyslové Muzeum*) contains a vast and varied collection of Art-Nouveau and avant-garde artistry from the 1890s–1930s, splendid Bohemian glasswork and

Above: *A statue of Smetana stands in the garden of the museum devoted to the composer.*

Above: *The National Museum is illuminated at night.*

St George's Convent

This beautiful medieval building (see p.27) is the setting for a permanent exhibition devoted to Mannerist Art from the reign of Rudolph II and Czech Baroque Art (c.1600–1800). Ferdinand Brokof is represented by some massive sculptures of Moorish warriors, as is his contemporary and rival, Matthias Braun. Jan Kupecký – whose work is dotted all over Prague – is a Bohemian artist whose vibrant paintings are also on show. The collection is arranged in chronological order and there is a fixed route for the viewer to follow through the building. The National Gallery's stunning collection of medieval painting and sculpture (1200–1550) has been moved to St Agnes' Convent (see p.36).

extensive displays of furniture, as well as interesting temporary exhibitions.

✉ 17 listopadu 2, opposite Rudolfinum, Josefov, ☎ 251 093 111, ⏱ 10:00–18:00 Tue–Sun, 🖋 admission charge, first Fri of month free, English or Czech audioguide included, 🍽 café, M Staroměstská.

National Museum

The vast Neo-Renaissance *Národní muzeum*, complete with glass dome, dominates the southern end of Wenceslas Square. Designed by Josef Schulz in 1890 in conscious emulation of the great museums of Paris and Vienna, the building is one of Prague's best testimonies to the Czech revival in the arts. The entrance is lined with figures, culminating in the personifications of History and Natural History, two of the museum's subjects. The building itself is the museum's chief highlight. Although the standard of temporary exhibitions has improved, the permanent exhibits are rather lacklustre.

✉ Václavské náměstí 68, Nové Město, ☎ 224 497 111, 🖥 www. nm.cz ⏱ daily 09:00–18:00 May–Sep, 09:00–17:00 Oct–Apr, closed first Tue every month, 🖋 70Kč, free first Mon of every month, M Muzeum (tram: 3, 9, 14).

Mucha Museum

An opportunity for a fascinating encounter with Alfons Mucha, one of the most influential artists of the Art Nouveau. The gorgeous exhibits include pastels, theatre posters, prints and photographs.

✉ Panská 7,

host of unpretentious places offering a range of cuisines, not just Czech but Chinese, Greek, Lebanese and more. Prices are cheap by Western standards, and you can expect to pay no more than around 500Kč for a three-course meal with wine in a good establishment. Be aware that a 23% tax, which should normally be included in the menu, is occasionally added to the total bill.

Vegetarians will not have as hard a time of it as they might have expected, given the Czech predilection for meat. Pizzerias and cafés with meat-free snacks abound, while two excellent restaurants for a more expensive meal out are U Cedru (*see* page 66) and La Provence (*see* page 64).

The places listed on the next few pages give an impression of what's available, but bear in mind that Prague's restaurants close down, or change management, with surprising regularity. For the latest recommendations, consult the 'Dining Out' section of the *Prague Post*, which gives reliable ratings. Credit cards are now widely accepted, at least at the more upmarket restaurants, but it's advisable to check beforehand.

> **Jaroslav Hašek**
> The creator of *The Good Soldier Svejk* was born in Prague in 1883. A prolific novelist, he published the four-volume *Svejk* – set at the time of the slow disintegration of the Austro-Hungarian empire – in 1920–23, and the novel was translated into English in 1930. Non-Czech readers who may be unfamiliar with Czech history might miss the understated nationalism that permeates the novel, but will still see the humour of the story in which the humble soldier Svejk blithely continues on his way, sowing confusion and disarray in the path of authority.
> **U Kalicha pub** is immortalized in the opening pages of the novel – it is here that Svejk is arrested for the assassination of Archduke Ferdinand.

Above: *Diners relax in the opulent surroundings of Obecní Dům, a splendid monument to Art-Nouveau architecture.*

Taxi! Waiter!
Natives of Prague would be among the first to admit that taxi drivers and waiters have given themselves a bad name. The arrival of capitalism and millions of tourists has had a dizzying effect on the city's taxi drivers, who have a reputation for overcharging and sharp practice. It is still safest to avoid using a taxi, but if one is used, agree a flat-rate fee before travelling and ask for a receipt on arrival. As for waiters, their service and politeness are excellent in many establishments, but there are still those whose instincts are to ignore or overcharge the customer.

Central Prague

• LUXURY

Ametyst

Intimate La Galleria restaurant on the ground floor of the Ametyst Hotel, where classical music serenades diners.

⊠ *Jana Masaryka 11, Prague 2,*
☎ *222 921 921,*
🖳 *www. hotelametyst.cz*
🖅 *mailbox@ hotelametyst.cz.*
🕑 *06:30–24:00 daily,*
M *Dejvická, Náměstí Míru.*

Arzenal

This glassware shop doubles as a gourmet Thai restaurant; diners have included actor Anthony Hopkins. The vegetarian and shellfish dishes are recommended.

⊠ *Valentinská 11, Prague 1,*
☎ *224 814 099,*
🖳 *www.arzenal.cz*

Hlučná samota

Traditional Czech restaurant, serving an impressive range of meat and fish dishes with rare flair and sophistication, at affordable prices.

⊠ *Záhřbská 14, Prague 2,*
☎ *222 522 839,*
🖳 *www.hlucna samota.cz*

La Provence

Delightfully furnished surroundings and freshly prepared food in generous portions evoke the atmosphere of southern France, even if it is snowing outside. Vegetarians can eat well here, and the service is prompt yet friendly. There's a nightclub and tapas bar upstairs, so it can get very noisy; reservations are advisable.

⊠ *Stuparská 9, Prague 1,* ☎ *296 826 155,* 🖅 *kontakt@ laprovence.cz*

💻 www.laprovence.cz
🕐 12:00–23:00 daily.

Bellevue

Regarded as one of the city's best restaurants. It is very popular for Sunday brunch from 11:00 to 15:00. Reservations are recommended.
⊠ Smetanovo nábřeží 18 (at Národní), Prague 1,
☎ 222 221 443 / 438,
🕐 daily 18:00–00:00.

Rybí trh

Located in the medieval Ungelt courtyard, behind the Týn Church, this excellent restaurant spoils diners with a superb choice of live or freshly imported fish and shellfish.
⊠ Týnský dvůr 5, Prague 1,
☎ 224 895 447,
💻 www.rybitrh.cz

• MID-RANGE
Ambiente

The third in the Ambiente group (the others are at Mánesova 59 and Americka 18) serves pleasing Italian fare, as well as light vegetarian meals.
⊠ Céletna 11, Prague 1,
☎ 224 230 244,
💻 www.ambi.cz
🕐 11:00–00:00 daily,
Ⓜ Náměstí Republiky.

Byblos

Tasty Lebanese and Middle Eastern dishes at affordable prices, especially if you opt for the fixed price mezze menu (minimum two persons).
⊠ Rybná 14, Prague 1,
☎ 221 842 121.

Radost FX

This famous bar and nightclub also excels in the culinary department. The menu includes Mexican and Thai specials, as well as vegetarian options and pasta dishes. Weekend brunch.
⊠ Běleradská 120, Prague 2,
☎ 224 254 776,
💻 www.radostfx.cz
🕐 11:30–04:00 daily,
Ⓜ IP Pavlova.

Reykjavik

Salted cod and tiger prawns in oyster sauce typify the varied menu of this leading seafood restaurant.
⊠ Karlova 20, Prague 1,
☎ 222 221 218,
📠 222 221 419,
💻 www.reykjavic.cz
🖅 info@reykjavic.cz
🕐 11:00–00:00 daily,
Ⓜ Staroměstská.

• BUDGET
Akropolis

Tasty, inexpensive Czech fare served until late.
⊠ Kubelíkova 27, Žižkov, Prague 3,
☎ 296 330 911,
💻 www.palacakropolis.cz
🖅 info@palacakropolis.cz
🕐 16:00–01:00 daily,
Ⓜ Jiřího z Poděbrad.

Downtown Café

This popular little eatery serves sandwiches, baguettes, cakes, etc. The coffee is good too.
⊠ Jungmannovo náměstí 21,

☎ 724 111 276,
🖥 www.downtown
cafe.cz

The Globe Bookstore and Coffeehouse

A favoured haunt of the expatriate American community, this small, lively, occasionally smoke-filled café offers a good range of mostly vegetarian soups, filled rolls and cakes, including delicious chocolate brownies. There's an equally small bookshop attached, with a rather eclectic collection of new and second-hand books.
✉ Pštrossova 6, Prague 1,
☎ 224 934 203,
🖥 www. globebookstore.cz
📧 globe@ globebookstore.cz
🕐 10:00–00:00 daily,
Ⓜ Národní Třída.

U Knihomola International Bookstore

Downstairs from the bookshop is a café offering light, French-style snacks and wine in a literary atmosphere.
✉ Mánesova 79, Prague 2,
☎ 222 729 348,
Ⓜ Jiřího z Poděbrad.

Hradčany

• *LUXURY*

Oživle drevo (Revived Wood)

For an interesting international dining experience try this restaurant situated within the Strahov Monastery. Expensive but delicious.
✉ Strahovské nádvoří 1, Prague 1 (tram 22, 23),
☎ 220 517 274,
📠 247 183 65,
🕐 11:00–23:00 daily,
🖥 www.ozivledrevo.cz

• *MID-RANGE*

Lví Dvůr

Delicious Czech specialities on the northern edge of the Prague Castle grounds above the Powder Bridge on the site of a former menagerie.
✉ U Pražského mostu 6/51 (tram 22, 23),
☎ 224 372 361,
📠 257 320 571,
🖥 www.lvidvur.cz
📧 lvidvur@lvidvur.cz
🕐 11:00–00:00 daily.

Northern Prague

• *LUXURY*

Hanavský pavilón

The Art-Nouveau pavilion affords panoramic views of the Vltava. Good game menu.
✉ Letenské sady 173, Letná,
☎ 233 323 641,
🕐 11:00–00:00
Ⓜ Malostranská to Chotkovy stop.

Letenský Zámeček

Take tea on the terrace, have sundowners with stunning views from the beer garden or dine in style inside the chateau.
✉ Letenské sady 341 (tram 12, 17),
☎ 233 378 200,
📠 233 378 199,
🖥 www. letenskyzamecek.cz
📧 office@ letenskyzamecek.cz
🕐 10:00–00:00 daily.

• MID-RANGE
U Cedru
(The Cedar)

Pink tablecloths and white napkins don't immediately conjure up images of the Orient, but the food quickly dispels any doubts. Lebanese cuisine is the speciality in this small, friendly restaurant; spicy falafels, stuffed vine leaves, smoked aubergine dip, tabbouleh and other (mostly) vegetarian starters are more than enough to satisfy hungry diners, and you probably won't manage a main course. The Arabic coffee is a good restorative. Evening reservations recommended.

⊠ Na Hutích 13, Dejvice, Prague 6, ☎ 233 342 974, 🕐 11:00–23:00 daily, M Dejvická.

Malá Strana
• LUXURY
Circle Line

The speciality of this brasserie is succulent shellfish, although

other international dishes are served; reservations are advisable.

⊠ Malostranské náměstí 12, Prague 1, ☎ 257 530 023, 🕐 12:00–23:00 Mon–Fri, 11:00–23:00 Sat and Sun.

U Malířů
(The Painter's)

This is the country's most expensive eating establishment, but also its only genuine gastronomic French restaurant. Ingredients are brought in from France twice a week for the French chef to create his *pièces*

Above: *The vaulted ceiling of Prague's most exclusive gourmet restaurant, U Malířů.*

What Sign are You?
Prague retains its ancient tradition of 'signing' its houses, a practice begun in the 14th century. Signs can be carved into gables, painted or etched into façades, or hung over doorways and windows. Many signs refer to the business of the house, as is often the case with pubs and restaurants, while others refer to a distinguishing feature of the building. Many of the signs are attractive and pictorially sophisticated; one of the small pleasures of wandering around the city is to spot the most interesting and unusual.

Lagerland

Pilsner lager is the best known Czech beer, brewed in the town of Plzeň (Pilsen) southwest of Prague. It has spawned hundreds of imitators worldwide and lent its name as the generic term for all of them. **Budweiser beer** is unrelated to the American beer of the same name, and is brewed in the town of Ceské Budějovice (Budweis) south of Prague. The Czechs produce beer in traditional ways, eschewing chemicals and growing their own hand-picked hops. Prague also has its own breweries, and some Prague bars brew their own beer.

Below: *A waiter serves the famous dark beer brewed at the pub U Fleků.*

de résistance, served in suitably elegant surroundings. Reservations essential. ⊠ *Maltézské náměstí 11, Prague 1,* ☎/📠 *257 530 000 /318* ⏰ *11:30–00:00 daily,* **M** *Malostranská.*

U Modré Kachničky
(The Blue Duck)

Just off Maltese Square in the Lesser Quarter, this is an intimate, romantic and beautifully decorated place that specializes in meat and game; reservations are essential for dinner. ⊠ *Nebovidská 6, Prague 1,* ☎/📠 *257 320 308/ 316 745,* 📟 *www.*

umodrekachnicky.cz ⏰ *12:00–16:00, 18:30–00:00 daily,* **M** *Malostranská.*

Nagoya

One of a number of Japanese restaurants making a splash in the city, Nagoya serves sushi, sashimi and tempura dishes to a consistently high standard. Reservations advised at weekends. ⊠ *Stroupežnického 23, Prague 5* ☎ *251 511 724* 📟 *www.nagoya.cz*

• *BUDGET*
U zeleného čaje
(Green Tea)

A tiny but very popular vegetarian café serving herbal teas and light snacks. You will need to get there very early, as there are only four tables. ⊠ *Nerudova 19, Malá Strana* ☎ *257 530 027,* ⏰ *11:00–19:30,* 📟 *www.gastroinfo.cz* **M** *Malostranská.*

68

Pubs and Beer Halls

Pubs and beer halls (*pivnice*) are all over Prague. Some are real 'locals' which don't really cater for visitors, while others go all out for the tourist trade: if in doubt stick to the centre of the city. As well as the excellent Czech ales and beers, many serve hearty Czech food in sizeable portions – the quality may be variable but quantity can always be guaranteed. Don't wait to be seated, but select your table and wait to be served. You may be joined by others if the place is crowded. Most bars and beer halls open from 10:00 until around 23:00.

Central Prague

U Fleků

Founded in medieval times, this large, popular *pivnice* is famous for the strong dark beer brewed on the premises.
☒ Křemencova 11,
☎ 242 934 019,
📠 242 934 805,
🕒 09:00–23:00 daily,
🖥 www.uflecku.cz
Ⓜ Národní Třída or Karlovo náměstí.

Jáma

This modern pub-style bar serves burgers, Tex-Mex and Czech specials, as well as draft beer.
☒ V Jámě 7, Prague 1, ☎ 224 222 383,
🖥 www.jamapub.cz

U Kalicha
(The Chalice)

Virtually all the food and drink and certainly all the decor is on a *Good Soldier Svejk* theme *see* panel, page 63). The pub is very popular with tourists, so if you fancy a drink it pays to get there early.
☒ Na bojišti 12–14, Prague 2,
☎ 296 189 600,
🖥 www.ukalicha.cz
🕒 11:00–23:00 daily,
Ⓜ Karlovo náměstí.

U zlatého tygra
(The Golden Tiger)

Crowded pub with literary connections and clientele.
☒ Husova 17,
☎ 222 221 111,
🖥 www.uzlateho tygra.cz
🕒 15:00–23:00 daily,
Ⓜ Staroměstská.

Malá Strana

Jo's Bar

Well-situated bar serving predominantly Mexican food to an appreciative American crowd. It is especially popular on Sundays.
☒ Malostranské náměstí 7,
☎ 257 533 342,
🕒 11:00–02:00 daily, (bar 11:00–05:00),
Ⓜ Malostranská.

Hradčany

U černého vola
(The Black Ox)

This extremely popular traditional Prague pub offers beer and pub snacks with lots of atmosphere.
☒ Loretánské náměstí 1,
☎ 220 513 481,
🕒 10:00–22:00 daily,
Ⓜ Malostranská to Pohořelec, tram 22.

Above: *Musicians of all ages and abilities gather on Charles Bridge to entertain the crowds.*

ENTERTAINMENT
Nightlife

Prague is a magical place at night – theatrical spotlights illuminate castles and bridges, lamps glow along cobbled streets, and music drifts throughout the city.

For a relaxing evening, take a walk across Charles Bridge where buskers provide the entertainment under the stars. Another great place for an evening stroll is through the Castle courtyards. From high atop the castle hill, you can see Prague sparkling below.

Prague's classical music is another option for evening entertainment. Music lovers are sure to enjoy the concerts performed in venues throughout the city (*see* pages 73 and 74). Performances such as Mozart's *Don Giovanni* at the Estates Theatre (*see* opposite page) are always well received.

There is also a wide selection of bars and taverns, most of which stay open until around 23:00, while clubs may stay open until 05:00 or 06:00 (*see* page 77).

Laterna Magika
Theatre
✉ Národní Třída 4, Nové Město, Prague 1
☎ 224 931 482
box office: 222 222 041
📠 222 222 039
🖥 www.laterna.cz
✉ pokladna@laterna.cz
🕐 10:00–20:00
Mon–Sat
Ⓜ Národní Třída

Theatre

As you would expect from the nation that elected a playwright to the presidency, Prague has a rich tradition in theatrical performance, which dates from the 1600s (although the city's first purpose-built theatre was only constructed in the late 1700s). Today's popular mainstream theatres may offer simultaneous transmission of a variety of languages and

(especially during the summer months) present a considerable number of English-language performances.

Laterna Magika is the most popular of the black-light theatre companies of Prague. This form of drama originated in the late 1950s and has since won for itself an increasingly devoted following. Its imaginative use of multiple-screen slide and film projection, dramatic use of light, and 'invisible' actors dressed entirely in black delights the packed audiences of tourists at whom the performances are now chiefly aimed. Prague's traditional folk puppetry also remains extremely popular (see page 42). A recent innovation has brought in 'live' actors to share the stage with their inanimate colleagues.

Prague's 'stone theatres' such as the **Vinohrady** stage impressive productions of serious drama, while mime traditions are still healthy. In the 1960s, **fringe theatres** sprang up as popular expressions of theatrical and political dissent (Havel worked in one) and they continue to stage experimental works. Tickets (best bought directly from the relevant box office) for all these sorts of productions are still relatively cheap by Western standards.

Estates Theatre

The **Estates Theatre** (*Stavovské divadlo*) was built in 1783 by Count Nostitz for the benefit of the large German community in this part of the city. It remains one of the finest neoclassical buildings in Prague. It was here that **Mozart** held the world premieres of *Don Giovanni* and *La*

Estates Theatre
✉ Ovocný trh 1, Staré Město
☎ 224 215 001
🖥 www.estates theatre.cz
✆ tickets@czech opera.cz
🕐 box office: Mon–Sun 10:00–18:00 and 45 minutes before evening performances, closed mid-Jul–mid-Aug
M Můstek

Below: *The neoclassical pediment and pillars of the historic Estates Theatre.*

Cosi fan tutte

National Theatre
✉ Národní 2,
Nové Město
☎ 224 901 448 (info)/
901 487 (tickets)
🖥 www.
narodni-divadlo.cz
✍ info@narodni-
divadb.cz
🕐 box office: Mon–Sun
10:00–18:00 and 45
minutes before evening
performances, closed
Jul and Aug
M Národní třída

Opposite: *The mon-
umental glass con-
struction of the
New Stage, com-
pleted in 1983,
forms part of the
National Theatre.*
Below: *The National
Theatre has a
unique blue roof
studded with stars.*

Clemenza di Tito, and 200 years later it was
used for interior shots in the film *Amadeus*
(income from which helped the authorities
renovate the building to its original splend-
our). The theatre also staged a light musical
comedy in 1834, one of the songs from
which (*Where is my home?*) later became
the Czech national anthem. The Estates
Theatre remains one of the principal venues
for theatre and opera in Prague, with an
emphasis, naturally enough, on Mozart.

Visitors and locals ensure that the Estates
Theatre is extremely well attended for
most performances, so it is wise to book
your seat in advance. As well as splendid
productions of opera and ballet, the theatre
is well worth seeing for its glorious interior.
The auditorium is lavishly decorated in
reds, creams and golds, with an elaborately
patterned ceiling. The boxes are the best
places to sit, as most of them provide uninterrupted views of the stage and the rest of
the audience – the theatre is small enough
for everyone to see and be seen.

National Theatre

The National Theatre (*Národní divadlo*) was
probably *the* symbol of what it meant to be
Czech in the 19th century. The
theatre was paid for by public
subscription, but days before
its official opening in 1881 it
was totally destroyed by fire.
Two years later a new building was completed under the
supervision of **Josef Schulz**
(who designed the National
Museum), and the first performance given there was

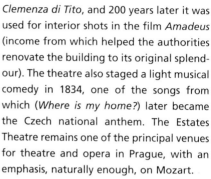

appropriately a Smetana opera. The theatre presents mainly Czech plays, opera and ballets.

The northern portal and the entire roofline of the theatre are covered in allegorical statuary, while the exterior of the topmost roof is coloured a vibrant blue dotted with silver stars (symbolizing the creative heights which all artists should aim for). All the major Czech artists of the period contributed work on the sumptuous interior decoration, which includes massive ceiling frescoes depicting the arts and a gorgeous stage curtain of reds and golds. In 1983 a controversial extension to the theatre called the **New Stage** (*Nová scéna*) was completed: love it or hate it, its series of gigantic glass boxes certainly catches the eye.

Music

Bohemia gave the world Dvořák and Smetana, and Prague took Mozart to its heart. The city's commitment to music undiminished, and encompasses everything from classical to contemporary ethnic. Be prepared to wade through the city's extensive listings to find what you want.

Classical music and **opera** are performed throughout the city in concert halls like the **Rudolfinum** (home of the Czech Philharmonic) and the **State Opera**, and in a host of elegant settings such as courtyards, squares, gardens, churches and palaces. The monthly programme is varied and extensive, and is augmented each year

---

Famous Czech Composers
Bedřich Smetana
(1824–84)
Antonín Dvořák
(1841–1904)
Leoš Janáček
(1854–1928)
Bohuslav Martinů
(1890–1959)

Rudolfinum
✉ Alšovo nábřeží 12, Staré Město, Prague 1
☎ 227 039 111
⌨ www.czech philharmonic.cz
✎ info@cfmail.cz
🕐 box office: 10:00–18:00 Mon–Fri and an hour before performances
Ⓜ Staroměstská

Above and opposite: *Prague continues to be a city in love with music and dance.*

from May to June by the **Prague Spring Music Festival** (*see* panel, page 75).

Prague's October **Jazz Festival** attracts musicians from around the world, and for the rest of the year the city has a thriving jazz scene in clubs and bars. The same is true for **rock** and **pop**.

State Opera

The terrible scar of Wilsonova (a five-lane highway) means that the State Opera (*Státní opera*) – east of the National Museum – now stands in noble isolation next to the brutalist former Federal Assembly. Built in 1888, it was called the New German Theatre and was intended to rival the Czech National Theatre which had just been built on the banks of the Vltava. Its wonderful façade – neoclassical in design – has six Corinthian columns supporting a pediment filled with a swirling frieze depicting Dionysus, the Greek god of wine, and Thalia, the classical muse of comedy. Inside, the magnificent auditorium is all gilt stucco and red plush, with many of the original paintings from the theatre's opening still in place – a night at the opera here would make for a memorable evening.

Smetana Hall, Municipal House

The **Smetana Hall**, named after the talented Czech composer, **Bedřich Smetana**, is an important part of Municipal House (*see* page 29). It is the city's largest concert venue and is the scene of the first concert in the annual Prague Spring Festival.

State Opera
⊠ Wilsonova 4,
Nové Město, Prague 1
☎ 224 227 266
🖳 www.opera.cz
✆ informace@
opera.cz
🕓 box office: 10:00–
17:30 Mon–Fri, 10:00–
12:00 and 13:00–17:30
Sat and Sun, and an
hour before performances; closed mid-Jul–
mid-Aug.
Ⓜ Můstek

Smetana Hall, Municipal House
⊠ Náměstí Republiky 5,
Nové Město, Prague 1
☎ 222 002 100
🖳 www.obecnidum.cz
✆ info@obecni-dum.cz
🕓 box office: 10:00–
18:00 daily
Ⓜ Náměstí Republiky
🍴 *see* Municipal
House, page 29

MUSIC, FESTIVALS & CINEMA

Festivals

The city's **festivals** and arts programmes are timed to the rhythm of the seasons, starting with the most famous of them all, the **Prague Spring Music Festival**. This extremely popular musical extravaganza includes orchestral concerts in Old Town Square and is accompanied by the flowers' colours returning to Prague's parks and gardens.

Another cultural festival is **Dance Prague** (*Tanec Praha*), an international festival of dance. Later in the year, the heat of summer brings out the city's street entertainers, while the **International Jazz Festival** is the first sign of autumn's arrival. December sees a proliferation of balls and dances, when the winter theatre season is also at its height. The balls take place from January to March in Prague's concert theatres and municipal halls.

Cinema

The Czech cinema is not what it once was. Today's film-makers seem content mostly to churn out sub-Hollywood-genre pictures, perhaps feeling rather overburdened by the expectations heaped on them and a heritage that stretches from the silent classics of the 1920s to the New Wave of the 1960s. Lower costs and a tendency to see Prague as a giant outdoor film set have meant that foreign productions have been filmed in the city (most famously *Amadeus*, directed by the Czech Miloš Forman, and the 1990s remake of *The Trial*). Domestic production, however, is in the doldrums.

<u>Festivals</u>

Prague Spring Music Festival
⊠ box office:
Hellichova 18,
Malá Strana
☎ 257 311 921
🖳 www.festival.cz
✆ festival@login.cz
🕘 May–Jun

Dance Prague
⊠ box office:
Husitská 24a, Prague 3
☎ 222 721 531
🖳 www.divadlo
ponec.cz
🕘 Jun–Jul

International Jazz Festival
⊠ box office:
u Bulhara 3, Prague 1
☎ 224 235 340/
777/701/588
🖳 www.jazzfestival
praha.cz
✆ info@prago
koncert.com
🕘 Oct

ENTERTAINMENT

Cinemas

Aero
✉ Biskupcova 31, Žižkov
☎ 271 771 349
🖳 www.kinoaero.cz

Evald
✉ Narodní třída 28,
☎ 221 105 225

Illusion
✉ Vinohradská 48
☎ 222 520 379

Lucerna
✉ Vodičkova 36, Nové Město
☎ 224 216 972

Mat Studio
✉ Karlova námesti 19, Nové Město
☎ 224 915 765
🖳 www.mat.cz

Bio Konvikt Ponrepo
✉ Bartolomějska 11, Staré Město
☎ 224 233 281

Below: *The home of Sparta Prague, the Czech Republic's most successful soccer team.*

Spectator Sports

American Football

Prague has two main teams – the **Prague Lions** and the **Prague Panthers**.

Prague Lions,
✉ Šrobárova 14, Prague 10,
☎/📠 267 915 511,
🖳 www.lions.cz
Prague Panthers,
play at Slavia Praha stadium (see below),
🖳 http://panthers.ambition.cz/

Football

AC Sparta Praha and **SK Slavia Praha** are the two most popular teams in Prague.

AC Sparta Praha,
✉ Stadion AC Sparta Praha, Milady Horákové 98,
☎ 220 570 323/296 111 400
📠 220 571 661,

🖳 www.sparta.cz
SK Slavia Praha,
✉ Stadion SK, Vladivostocká 2,
☎/📠 257 213 290,
🖳 www.slavia.cz

Horse Racing

Trots, steeplechases and hurdles take place at **Velka Chuchle**, Prague's main racecourse.
✉ Radotínská 69,
☎ 242 447 031,
🕓 steeplechases and hurdles Sun afternoons from 14:00 May–Oct, trots on Thu throughout the year,
M Smíchovské nádraží, then bus 129, 172, 241, 244.

Ice Hockey

Czechs generally love ice hockey and have won the World Championships several times. **Sparta Praha** is just one of the many popular teams.
🖳 www.hokej.cz
Sparta Praha,
✉ Za elektrárnou 419, Holešovice,
☎ 266 727 443,
🖳 www.hcsparta.cz
M Nádraží Holešovice.

Nightclubs
Staré Město
**Karlovy Lázně
(Charles Baths)**
Four different dance floors in the old municipal baths near Charles Bridge.

✉ Smetanovo Nábřežíy 198, Prague 1
☎ 222 220 502,
🖥 www.karlovylazne.cz
🕘 09:00–05:00,
M Staroměstská.

Lávka
Situated on an island overlooking the river, castle and Charles Bridge. The outdoor dancing venue is popular in summer.

✉ Novotného lávka 1, ☎ 221 082 288, 🖥 www.lavka.cz
🕘 21:00–04:00 daily,
M Staroměstská.

Malá Strana
Jo's Garáž
Loud, popular disco in a cellar under Jo's Bar (see page 69).

✉ Malostranské náměstí 7,
☎ 257 533 342,
🕘 21:00–05:00 daily,
M Malostranská.

Nové Město
Lucerna Music Bar
Live gigs and dance nights in an early 20th-century auditorium. One of the best gig venues in Prague.

✉ Vodičova 36,
☎ 224 217 108,
🖥 www.musicbar.cz
🕘 20:00–03:00,
M Můstek.

Vyšehrad
Radost FX
Pleasant dance club. Also has a large bar and café upstairs. Great cocktails.

✉ Bělehradská 120, Vinohrady,
☎ 224 254 776,
🕘 21:00–06:00,
M IP Pavlova.

Northern Prague
Mecca
Located in a converted factory, this is one of Prague's most popular clubs.

✉ U Průhonu 3, Holešovice, ☎ 283 870 522,
🖥 www.mecca.cz
M Nádraží Holešovice to U Průhonu, tram 12, 14.

Above: *The Karlovy Lázně dance club is the largest in eastern Europe.*

<u>**Gay Clubs and Restaurants**</u>

Bar 21
✉ Rúmska 21, Prague 2
☎ 724 254 048
🕘 11:00–00:00 daily
M Náměstí Mirů

Fajn Bar
✉ Dittríchova 5, Prague 2
☎ 224 917 409

Friends Bar
✉ Bartolomejska 11, Prague 1
☎ 224 236 772
🖥 www.friends-prague.cz
🕘 16:00–03:00 daily
M Národní třída

Pinocchio
✉ Selfertova 3, Žižkov
☎ 222 710 773
🖥 pinocchio@seznam.cz
🕘 15:00–06:00
M Hlavní nádraží

Above: *Magnificent views from one of the thermal baths at Karlovy Vary.*
Opposite*:*
Mariánské Lázně has many lovely buildings from the late 19th century.

Day Trips From Prague
The countryside around Prague has in some ways changed very little over the years: villages nestle in the folds of the forested hills, castles keep watch over the valleys, and wistfully elegant spa towns still provide their healing waters. Many of these places are accessible by coach excursion direct from Prague city centre and can be seen in a day or an afternoon. Alternatively, if you have your own transport, these destinations are well signposted and make for a pleasant drive through the Bohemian countryside.

EXCURSIONS
The Spa Towns
Karlovy Vary

More famously known by its former name of Karlsbad, Karlovy Vary can be reached by coach excursion and scheduled train or bus. Since the early 1500s the town has depended for its income on the healing properties of its 12 hot mineral springs. Its heyday was in the century before World War I, when the rich and the famous 'took the waters' in the elegant surroundings of the fashionable town: at one time or another **Beethoven**, **Karl Marx** and **Edward VII** all stayed here. Karlovy Vary's fortunes have faded since then, but it still provides cures to a vast public. In the summer months, there are delightfully bourgeois concerts, cultural events and racecourse meetings.

Much of the pleasure of Karlovy Vary consists in wandering among its *belle époque* hotels and villas, which drape themselves over the wooded hillsides upon which the town is built – see, especially, **Sadova ulice**. The vast **Imperial Sanatorium** stands aloof on its hilltop site, watched by the bronze chamois at **Deer Leap** (*Jelení skok*) across the valley – accessible on foot and by funicular railway.

Kilian Ignaz Dientzenhofer's Church of Mary Magdalene (*sv. Maří Magdalény*) – built in 1736 – should on no account be missed; neither should the 19th-century **Russian Orthodox Church** with its gold onion domes. Churches of all denominations have been built here to serve

the town's cosmopolitan population. The Corinthian-columned **Mill Colonnade** designed by Josef Zítek (architect of Prague's original National Theatre) is the town's 19th-century *pièce de résistance*.

Mariánské Lázně

Formerly known as Marienbad, this spa town is smaller and younger than Karlovy Vary. The spa was founded in the early 19th century, although its 40 springs were known about as far back as the 1600s. Superbly located amid densely wooded hills, its late development has resulted in a delightful architectural uniformity: most buildings date from the second half of the 19th century. Pride of place goes to Mariánské Lázně's great cast-iron **Colonnade**, which was finished in 1889 – people taking the cure still stroll under its glass canopy. Like Karlovy Vary, it is fun just to wander through the town to admire the immaculate houses and wonder what it might be like to live in them. Most of Mariánské Lázně's villas and hotels have some sort of literary association: **Goethe** stayed at what is now the **City Museum** in 1823, and is commemorated in **Goethe Square** (*Goethovo náměstí*). **Franz Kafka** spent the summer here in 1916, while other writers and musicians who took the spring waters include **Gogol**, **Ibsen**, **Kipling**, **Twain**, **Bruckner**, **Wagner** and **Weber**.

The forested countryside around the town also provides some lovely walks.

Karlovy Vary
Location: Map A–A3
Distance from
Prague: 140km (85 miles) west of Prague

Kur-Info
✉ Vřídelní kolonada
☎ (017) 322 40 97
📠 (017) 322 93 12
🖥 www.karlovyvary.cz
📧 lkurinfo@ plz.pvtnet.cz

Mariánské Lázně
Location: Map A–A4
Distance from
Prague: 170km (105 miles) west of Prague

Infocentrum KaSS
✉ Dum Chopin, Hlavní 47, 353 01, Mariánské Lázne
☎ 354 622 474
📠 354 625 892
🕐 daily 09:00–12:00, 13:00–18:00
🖥 www.marienbad.com
📧 infocentrum@ marianskelazne.cz

Karlstein
Location: Map A–D4
Distance from
Prague: 25km (16 miles) southwest
✉ Statni hrad Karlštein
☎ (0311) 681 617
📞 (0311) 681 211
🖥 www.hradkarlstejn.cz
📧 karlstejn@stc.npu.cz

Konopiště
Location: Map A–E5
Distance from
Prague: 40km (25 miles) southeast
☎ (0317) 728 808
🖥 www.konopiste.com
📧 compro@compro.cz

Křivoklát
Location: Map A–C4
Distance from
Prague: 46km (29 miles) west of Prague
✉ Státní hrad Křivoklát
☎ (0313) 558 440
🖥 www.krivoklat.cz
📧 krivoklat@stc.npu.cz

Bohemian Castles

Karlstein

In the best traditions of fairytale, Karlstein (*Karlštejn*) Castle is set on a wooded promontory overlooking a river, and comprises a series of turreted towers and battlements within a crenellated wall that strides down the hillside. It makes no difference that what you see is mostly 19th-century reconstruction and that little remains of the original 14th-century fortress built by Charles IV to house the crown jewels. It's great fun, and children in particular are pleased with the whole experience.

Konopiště

Konopiště Castle is set in extensive parkland on the site of a 13th-century fortress. The largely 19th-century structure still bears traces of Baroque construction, most particularly in its great gate sculpted by **Matthias Braun** in 1725. The castle has large collections of hunting trophies plus a good deal of arms, armour and porcelain. From 1897, Konopiště was **Archduke Ferdinand**'s favourite retreat. Heir to the Austrian throne and married to a Czech, it was his assassination in Sarajevo in 1914 that sparked off World War I.

Křivoklát

Křivoklát Castle's similarity to Karlstein is due to **Josef Mocker**, who restored both castles in the 19th century. Much of the original 13th-century Přemyslid hunting lodge remains, as do signs of Charles IV's occupation.

Křivoklát's dominant feature is its **Great Tower**, which is 42m (130ft) high. There is also a splendid Gothic chapel and a dungeon prison with a torture museum.

White Mountain

On the western edge of Greater Prague – accessible by tram 22 – White Mountain (*Bílá hora*) is the site of the famous battle of the **Thirty Years War**, which decided the fate of Bohemia for the next 300 years. In the 16th century, a royal hunting park and lodge were constructed on what was to be the battle site a century later. Star (*Hvězda*) hunting lodge is so called because it was built in the shape of a six-pointed star, its steeply sloping roof emphasizing every angle of the building. Constructed in 1556, it was restored in the 1950s and now houses a small museum dedicated to the writer **Alois Jirásek** and the painter **Mikoláš Aleš**. But the unusual building is itself the best exhibit. The sand-coloured walls of its simple and dignified exterior are nicely complemented by the large red-tiled roof. Inside, it is beautifully decorated with elegant frescoes and stucco detailing.

Above: *A stone cairn marks the site of the Battle of the White Mountain (*Bílá hora*) fought between Catholic and Protestant forces in 1620.*
Opposite: *Karlstein Castle was founded in the 14th century by Charles IV to protect his royal treasures.*

Břevnov Monastery

East of the park and just a few minutes' walk away is **Břevnov Monastery** (*Břevnovský klášter*). A Benedictine Abbey was founded here in the 10th century, but most of the present monastery is the work of **Christoph** and **Kilian Ignaz Dientzenhofer**. The outstanding building of the complex is the **Church of St Margaret**, which was built by Christoph Dientzenhofer in 1715. This is a *tour de force* of intersecting ovals, in its floor plan and its exterior façade. It is one of the

---

White Mountain
Location: Map A–D3
M Dejvická

Břevnov Monastery
✉ Praha 6, Marketská
☎ 220 406 111
🚌 guided tours 10:30, 13:00, 14:30 and 16:00 Sat and Sun, 2 Apr – 7 Oct, 10:00 and 14:00 Sat and Sun 8 Oct – 1 April
🖰 klaster@brevnov.cz

most invigorating examples of Prague Baroque. The remains of the original 10th-century church can be seen in the crypt. The monastery meeting room – with its 18th-century frescoed ceiling – is also worth seeing.

Kutná Hora

Established in the 13th century, this mining town grew to become second only to the capital in wealth and importance. Until they gave out in the 16th century, the town's deposits of silver made the Bohemian king Europe's richest monarch. Much of the money was used to construct remarkable buildings, such as the **Church of St Barbara** (*sv. Barbora*), which was begun in the late 14th century by **Peter Parler**'s workshop. The church – dedicated to the patron saint of miners – has been described as one of the most beautiful in Europe. It rises majestically in an array of flying buttresses to three graceful tent-like spires, in an unsurpassed display of Bohemian Gothic wizardry. The unforgettable exterior is matched by a superb interior lit by intricately traced windows. It has a tremendous vaulted ceiling emblazoned with coats of arms and several Late Gothic wall murals.

On the road lined with Baroque statuary that leads up to the cathedral, **Kilian Ignaz Dientzenhofer**'s monumental **Ursuline convent** looks out across the valley. Kutná Hora's **Italian Court** (*Vlašský dvůr*) dates from the time of Václav II. Now the town hall, for centuries it was the mint which produced the Prague Groschen, a silver coin that was at one time in circulation all over Europe. A guided tour takes tourists

---

Kutná Hora
Location: Map A–F4
Distance from Prague: 70km (45 miles) east of Prague

Infocentrum ✉
Palackeho náměstí 377
☎ (0327) 512 378
📠 (0327) 512 873
💻 www.kutnahora.cz

Church of St Barbara
🕘 09:00–11:30 and 13:00–16:00 daily Apr–Oct, 09:00–11:30 and 14:00–15:30 Tue–Sun Nov–Mar, 🎟 30Kč

Italian Court
✉ Havlíčkovo náměstí 552, ☎/📠 (0327) 512 873, 💻 www.kutnahora.cz
📧 guide@mu.kutnahora.cz
🎟 50Kč (guided tour)

Mining Museum
✉ Barborská
☎ (0327) 512 159
🕘 09:00–12:00 and 13:00–17:00 Tue–Sun Apr–Oct, 🎟 100Kč (guided tour)

around Kutná Hora's Art-Nouveau chapel. The **Mining Museum** allows visitors to explore part of the medieval workings which spread right under the village.

As you wander through the streets, look out for the **Gothic fountain** and **plague column**, and the **Stone House**, the façade of which is carved with decorative relief work

Lidice

The modern village of Lidice is close to Prague, but it should be noted that it is a destination which is not likely to be suitable for younger children. After the assassination of *Reichsprotektor* Reinhard Heydrich in May 1942, the old village of Lidice was chosen by the Nazis as an example and a warning. On 10 June, all the men of the village were shot and the women were taken to Ravensbrück concentration camp. The 89 children were taken to similar camps. The village was totally destroyed. The Nazis boasted that they would erase the name of Lidice from the map, but in fact quite the opposite occurred. Towns and villages around the world changed their name to Lidice to preserve the memory of those who died: thus did Lidice live on.

The main street of the new village is called 10 Cervna 1942 (10 June 1942), after the date of the atrocity. It leads to the memorials that mark the location of the old village, which is now just a grass-covered field. There is a small, harrowing museum that has original SS film footage of the burning village.

Lidice is a disturbing place, but visitors may find there a little hope to take away with them.

Lidice
Location: Map A–D3
Distance from Prague: 19km (12 miles) northwest

Lidice Memorial Museum
☎ (0312) 253 063
🕐 08:00–17:00
💰 50Kč
💻 www.lidice-memorial.cz
✉ lidice@quick.cz

Opposite: *The Benedictine monastery of Břevnov was founded in AD993. In the 18th century, architects Christoph and Kilian Ignaz Dientzenhofer rebuilt the complex in the then fashionable Baroque style.*
Below: *The Church of St Barbara at Kutná Hora.*

Above: *Trams are the best way to get around the city.*

Sightseeing

Many of Prague's sights are concentrated within quite a small central area, and the best way of getting your bearings is simply to explore on foot – in fact, Charles Bridge is accessible only to pedestrians. Comfortable flat shoes are best for walking along the cobbled streets. Watch out for the trams, which run in the centre of the road in both directions. If you want to cross the city more quickly, or if the streets leading up to Prague Castle from Lesser Quarter Square prove too steep, the public transport system is cheap, efficient and reliable. It comprises a metro system as well as a network of trams and buses. Be aware that during the morning and evening rush hours, between 06:30 and 08:30 and from 15:00 to 18:30, public transport gets very crowded.

Best Times to Visit

Every season has its attraction. You may want your visit to coincide with a particular event, such as the Prague Spring Music Festival, which begins in the middle of May, or the Christmas festivities in December. Prague enjoys a temperate climate, which means that while summers are generally hot, **winter** (Nov–Mar) can be bitterly cold and the skies are grey, which can give the city a forlorn look. On the other hand, snow enhances the beauty of the buildings and there can be no more magical place than Prague at Christmas. **Spring** is a delightful time – trees are starting to bud and the days are becoming warmer. **Summer** brings city life outside and attracts greater crowds. Finding a room or a place to eat at this time can be problematic and so advance booking is strongly advised.

Tourist Information

Since 1989, there has been a proliferation of private tourist agencies. Standards and range of services vary as anywhere else, but there is no shortage to choose from. The **Prague Information Service** (PIS), ⊠ Betlémské náměstí 2, Prague 1, ☎ 221 714 319/12 444, 📞 222 220 700, 🖥 www.pis.cz 🖰 tourinfo@pis.cz provides maps, advice, listings, and guided sightseeing tours. Many agencies employ English-speaking staff, but a knowledge of German is handy. **American Express**, ⊠ Václavské náměstí 56, ☎ 222 800 251, offers a wide range of travel services. **Czech Tourism**, ⊠ Vínhoradská 46, Prague 1, PO Box 32, 12044, Prague 2, ☎ 221 580 111, 📞 224 247 516, 🖰 info@czechtourism.cz 🖥 www.visitczechia.cz Travel tickets, car rental, exchange office. **Cedok** ⊠ Václavské náměstí 53, Prague 1,

☎ 224 224 926. Tours, river cruises and sight-seeing trips.

✉ Rytířská 16, ☎ 224 224 237, ℱ 222 246 394. Trips through Bohemia and abroad; exchange.

Pragotur, ✉ Na příkopě 20, ☎ 224 482 562, ✆ tourinfo@pis.cz

Prague Information Service branches, **Lucerna Passage** ✉ Vodičková 36, Prague 1; ✉ Old Town Hall, Staroměstské náměstí 1, ✉ Malostranská mostecká vž (summer only). Tourist information and brochures.

Thomas Cook, ✉ Národní 28, Prague 1 ☎ 221 105 371. Business travel, tourist programmes, currency exchange.

General information: Czech Embassy, ✉ 6 Kensington Palace Gardens, London W8 4QY, ☎ (020) 7243 1115, ℱ (020) 7727 9654.

Embassies and Consulates

Canada: ✉ Muchova 6, Prague 6, ☎ 272 101 800, ℱ 272 101 890.

Republic of South Africa: ✉ Ruská 65, Prague 10, ☎ 267 311 114, ℱ 267 311 395.

UK: ✉ Thunovská 14, Prague 1, ☎ 257 402 111, ℱ 222 243 652.

USA: ✉ Tržiště 15, Prague 1, ☎ 257 530 663, ℱ 257 530 920.

Entry Requirements

To enter the Czech Republic, visitors must have a passport (valid for at least six months beyond the return date). Visitors from the EU, USA and Canada do not require a visa; other nationals are advised to check at their nearest Czech embassy or consulate.

Customs

Residents of EU countries are allowed to bring into the Czech Republic personal effects for use during their visit in the following quantities: 2 litres of wine, 1 litre of spirits, 200 cigarettes (or the equivalent in cigars or tobacco), and for hunting, 1000 shotgun pellets or 50 rifle bullets. These quantities can be exported duty free, in addition to gifts up to the value of 3000Kč and any goods purchased with foreign currency in a Tuzex shop. Keep receipts as proof of purchase. Information from General Customs Head Office, ✉ Sokolovská 22, ☎ 261 331 111.

Health Requirements

Your hotel should be able to contact the local doctor or, in an emergency, call the ambulance (☎ 155). Emergency medical attention is free for foreign visitors from countries that have reciprocal health agreements with the Czech Republic, otherwise all non-emergency treatment must be paid for on the spot. You should take out insurance. Obtain a receipt for your insurance claim. There is a 24-hour emergency

service for foreign visitors at the Diplomatic Health Centre (*Nemocnice Na Homolce*), ✉ Roentgenova 2, ☎ 252 922 146. Some **pharmacies** (*lékárna*) stay open after regular business hours. A 24-hour pharmacy is Lekarna U Andelaat ✉ Stefanikova 6, Prague 5, ☎ 257 320 918, **M** Anděl. Emergency **dental** treatment is provided at European Dental Center ✉ Václavské náměstí 33, ☎ 224 228 984. The **First Aid Centre** (*Služba prbní pomoci*) at ✉ Palackého 5, ☎ 224 946 981, gives basic remedies. If you take prescribed medication, bring an adequate supply with you, as equivalents may be difficult or impossible to obtain.

Getting There

By air: The easiest and quickest way to travel to Prague is by plane. The city has good airline connections with many European and North American cities, although travellers from Australia, New Zealand and South Africa are not served directly. Direct flights from London operate about four times daily, and flight time is around two hours. The cheapest standard fare is an Apex return, which must be reserved at least 14 days in advance. The national carrier, Czech Airlines (CSA), also flies from Manchester to Prague up to six times a week. Discounted flights are advertised in the UK Sunday newspapers. In peak season flights are booked up several weeks in advance.

By road: If bringing your own car, you must have your valid driving licence (an Inter national Driving Licence is advisable), vehicle registration card and an international insurance certificate (green card). You also need replacement bulbs, a hazard warning triangle and a first-aid kit, and a national identity sticker. The minimum age for driving is 18.

By rail: Prague has very good rail connections with the rest of Europe – all the major capitals are linked by train. The main station is the Hlavní nádraží on Wilsonova.

What to Pack

Bring something warm such as a sweater or jacket and a raincoat as it rains throughout the year. From May–Aug the days are long and hot. Jun–Jul is the hottest. Cool cotton clothes are essential and an umbrella is useful to ward off sudden summer showers. Flat, comfortable shoes are best for Prague's hills and cobbled streets. The wettest months are from Oct–Nov, when temperatures begin to drop. Snow usually starts in Nov/Dec, and continues through Jan and Feb; these months can get bitterly cold.

Money Matters

Currency: The unit of

currency in the Czech Republic is the crown (*koruna*), abbreviated Kč. It is divided into 100 hellers (h). Bank notes come in denominations of 20, 50, 100, 200, 500, 1000, 2000 and 5000Kč; coins as 10h, 20h, 50h, and 1, 2, 5, 10, 20 and 50Kč. Import and export of crowns is restricted to 200,000Kč; notes can be converted back into western currency at the airport (keep your exchange receipts).

Currency Exchange: Money can be changed at most banks, hotels and currency exchange offices. Banks generally offer the best commission, though the queues are often long. There are many small, privately run bureaux de change all over the city. Many charge large commissions, or their rate of exchange is disadvantageous. Some exchange bureaux are open 24 hours. **Never** use the black market; it is illegal and you run the very real risk of being cheated.

Travellers' Cheques: The safest way of carrying money is in the form of travellers' cheques – Thomas Cook and American Express are the best known. Cheques must first be changed into crowns, as they are not accepted by shops or restaurants.

Credit Cards: Credit cards such as Visa, Mastercard (Access) and American Express are becoming widely accepted and you'll be able to use plastic in the more expensive hotels, shops and restaurants.

Tipping: Tipping is not generally required but is greatly appreciated if the service has been particularly attentive.

VAT: Value added tax (sales tax) of either 5 or 19% is normally included in the total cost; essential food is exempt from VAT.

Transport

Air: Prague's international airport, Ruzyně, 15km (9 miles) northwest of the city centre,

Tickets and Passes:

Tickets are uniform across the public transport system and must be bought before you make your journey. Tickets must always be stamped or punched in the machines, otherwise they are invalid. Ticket inspectors make periodic checks and levy hefty on-the-spot fines on travellers without a valid ticket. Single tickets (*jízdenky*) are available throughout the city from tobacconists (*tabák*), street kiosks, newsagents, hotels and some shops, or they may be bought from the orange machines at some bus and tram stops and inside metro stations (exact change is required). Children under six travel free, and between six and 15 years at half price. If you want to avoid the problem of not having the right change for the single-journey ticket, or if you plan to use public transport extensively, then a multi-day tourist pass (*turistická síová jízdenka*) is an excellent investment. These passes, available for periods of one, three, seven or 15 days, can be bought from tourist offices and offer unlimited travel on buses, trams and trains. They do not need to be validated in the machines, but you should sign and date the ticket before using it.

Good Reading
• **Bruce Chatwin**, *Utz* (1989). Compelling tale of an obsessive collector in postwar Prague.
• **Slavenka Drakulič**, *How We Survived Communism and Even Laughed* (1992). Feminist perspective of life under the communist regime.
• **Timothy Garton Ash**, *The People: The Revolution of 89* (1990). Eyewitness account of an extraordinary year in Europe.
• **Jaroslav Hašek**, *The Good Soldier Svejk and his Fortunes in the World War*. Picaresque tale of the Czech Republic's most infamous fictional character.
• **Václav Havel**, *Living in Truth* (1989). Celebrates the playwright-president's fight for freedom of thought.

has 24-hour exchange facilities, car rental, a duty-free shop, restaurant, post office and left-luggage office. It is linked to the centre by CEDAZ minibus shuttle and regular bus service; buses usually leave every hour from the arrivals building. Taxis are readily available.

Road: A motorway toll coupon costing 100Kč per car (valid for ten days) is essential for travel within the Czech Republic. It can be bought at Czech border crossings.

Road conditions: Outside main towns roads are relatively free of traffic and well signposted, but conditions in winter can be treacherous.

Driving regulations: In urban areas, the speed limit is 50kph (31mph), on dual and single carriageways 90kph (56mph), and on motorways 130kph (80mph). Children under 12 are not allowed in front. The permissible blood alcohol level for drivers is 0.00 per ml, and penalties are severe.

Car rental: Considering Prague's extensive public transport, its confusing web of one-way streets and its shortage of parking, driving in the city is not really viable. If you want to hire a car for day trips from Prague, one of the cheapest companies is **Esocar** at ✉ Husitská 58, Prague 3, ☎ 283 892 211–4. More expensive agencies include: **Avis**, ✉ Klimentská 46, Prague 1, ☎ 221 851 225; Airport Ruzyně, ✉ Prague 6, ☎ 231 667 39, **Budget** at the Hotel InterContinental, ✉ Parížská, ☎ 224 889 995, or **Europcar**, ✉ Parížská 28, ☎ 224 811 290.

Taxi: Taxi drivers have a reputation for tourist exploitation so use taxis with caution. A minimum charge applies as soon as you step into the taxi; after that there is a legally fixed rate per

kilometre. If you suspect you've been overcharged, ask for a receipt (*potrzeni*), which must be given by law if requested.
Rail: Express trains (*Rychlíl*) travel to major towns. Slow passenger trains (*Osobnýs*) are very slow and usually stop at every station. All tickets can be purchased in advance. The metro system is extremely smooth and easy to use. It has three lines, A, B and C. Purchase a metro map from the tourist office to help you plan your route. Maps are on display in some of the larger metro stations, and there's a metro map inside trains above each door. Metro entrances are signalled by a letter 'M' against an inverted triangle, in green (line A), yellow (line B) or red (line C). Doors open and close automatically. During the journey, a recorded message in Czech announces the next

station. With a single ticket you can change between lines as many times as you like within one hour, but once you leave the underground system your ticket becomes invalid. Once at your stop, follow the exit (*Výstup*) sign to find your way out.
Buses: The city's main bus terminal is near Metro Florenc, on the eastern edge of New Town. It serves all international routes as well as long-distance journeys within the Czech Republic. A timetable is posted at the station.
Trams and buses: You use the same single tickets for the trams as for the metro and bus networks. Once aboard the tram, validate your ticket in one of the brown machines; insert your ticket and pull the lever towards you. Tickets are valid for one journey only. Tram timetables are posted at tram stops.

The stop at which you are standing is underlined, and all the stations below it are where the tram is going next. Travelling by tram is an excellent way of getting around. The service is frequent and reliable, and reaches into all parts of the city, offering cheap sightseeing possibilities. At night, a limited number of trams runs every 40 minutes from around midnight to 05:00.
The city's bus system covers the more outlying suburbs. Buses are noisy and dirty, and for the most part are kept well out of Prague centre. The procedure for buying and validating tickets applies as for trams and the underground.

Business Hours
Museums, galleries, and tourist sites usually ⏰ 09:00 or 10:00 to 17:00 or 18:00, Tue–Sun, closed Mon. Some remain open throughout the

year, but others close in winter, so check with the tourist office. Most **banks** ☉ 09:00–17:00 Mon–Fri, and are usually closed for an hour between 12:00 and 14:00. The *Komercní banka* at ✉ Na příkopě 33 ☉ until 19:00 weekdays and 09:00–14:00 Sat. **Post offices** ☉ 08:00–18:00 Mon–Fri, 08:00–12:00 Sat. **Food shops** ☉ 06:00 until 18:00 Mon–Fri, and 07:00–12:00 Sat; other shops generally ☉ 09:00–18:00 Mon–Fri, 09:00–12:00 Sat. Many shops in the centre of Prague stay open until 19:00 or later, and Tesco is open on Sundays. Many **pubs** and **restaurants** close at 22:00 or 23:00.

Time Difference

Prague is one hour ahead of GMT.

Communications

The general post office (*Hlavní pošta*) at ✉ Jindřišská 14, near Wenceslas Square, ☎ 221 131

111, ☉ 24 hours. Other post offices are at ✉ Kaprova 12, Josefská 4, Hybernská 15 and at Prague Castle.
Faxes can also be sent from the main post office.

Electricity

The standard 220 volts AC is used.

Weights and Measures

Prague uses the metric system.

Health Precautions

No inoculations are required.
Ambulance transport, ☎ 155.
Diplomatic Health Centre for Foreigners, ✉ Na Homolce, Roentgenova 2, ☎ 257 225 040. Doctors speak English and German.
Emergency Dental Treatment, ✉ Palackého 5, ☎ 224 946 981.

Personal Safety

Compared with other cities in Europe,

Prague has a low crime rate and assaults are rare. The biggest problem comes from pickpockets, who are rife in summer in the main tourist areas and on the trams and metro. Take sensible precautions such as carrying only as much money as you need, leaving your passport and tickets in your hotel safe, and noting down credit card and travellers' cheque numbers. Women travelling alone should avoid Wenceslas Square and the area around the main railway station at night.

Emergencies

If you have been robbed, go to the police. Your insurance company will require a police report. Police headquarters: ✉ Bartolomějská 6, Old Town, ☎ 224 131 111.
Police, ☎ 158.
City Police, ☎ 156.
Ambulance, ☎ 155.

Fire, ☎ 150.

Road, ☎ 154.

Lost Credit Cards,
Amex ☎ 222 800 222;
Diner's Club ☎ 267
197 450; Visa,
Mastercard/Eurocard
☎ 272 771 111.

Language

The national language is Czech, and any attempt at speaking it will be appreciated. If you find it too daunting, a knowledge of German is helpful. English is increasingly understood among the younger generation (*see* panel, page 62).

Useful Contacts

Airport, General information, ☎ 239 007 007;
Departures/arrivals, ☎ 220 113 314; 24 hour service, ☎ 220 111 111, 🖥 www.csa.cz

American Center for Culture and Commerce,
✉ Hybernská 7a,
☎ 224 231 085; exhibitions, newspapers, library and business reference service.

Bohemia Ticket International,
✉ Malé náměstí 13,
☎ 224 227 832,
📠 224 218 167;
✉ Na příkopě 16,
☎ 224 215 031; tickets can be bought in advance, though it is more expensive than the box office;
🖥 www.bohemiaticket.cz

British Council, ✉ Národní 10, ☎ 221 991 111, temporary exhibitions, library, resources centre and satellite Sky TV news.

Customs Office Headquarters,
☎ 224 816 256.

Czech Railways Travel Agency (*Ceské Dráhy – Cestovní Kancelař*),
✉ nábřeži Ludvika Svobody 1225, Prague 1, ☎ 412 503 113,
🖥 www.cd.cz

French Institute, ✉ Stepánská 35, ☎ 224 401 011, screen classic French films and have a popular café.

Lost and Found,
✉ Karolíny Svetlé 5,
Prague 1,
☎ 224 235 085.

Useful Words and Phrases

letiště • airport
účet • bill/check
autobus • bus
auto • car
hrad • castle
kostel • church
zavřeno • closed
vchod • entrance
prominte • excuse me
vychod • exit
průvodce • guide
nemocnice • hospital
kolik to stojí? • how much?
nerozumim • I don't understand
rozumim • I understand
informace • information
toalety • lavatory
ztráty a nálezy • lost property
otevřeno • open
pas • passport
vízum • visa
benzin • petrol
lékárna • pharmacy
policie • police
pošta • post office
nádraží • railway station
známka • stamp
ulice • street
jizdenka, vstupenka • ticket
děkuji • thank you
dnes • today
zitra • tomorrow
jízda • tour
vlak • train
tramvaj • tram
kdy • when
kdo • who
kam • where
ano/ne • yes/no
včera • yesterday

INDEX OF SIGHTS

GENERAL INDEX

🖥 *www.mucha.cz*
☎ *221 451 333,*
🕐 *Open daily
10:00-18:00,*
👗 *admission charge.*
M *Můstek.*

Prague City Museum

Muzeum hlavního města Prahy inhabits an 1890s Neo-Renaissance house and contains an eclectic display relating to the city, including a 20 m² model of Prague made in 1834 by Antonín Langweil.
✉ *Na poříčí 52, Prague 8, Nové Město,* ☎ *224 816 772,* 🖥 *www.muzeumprahy.cz* 🕐 *09:00–18:00 Tue–Sun.*
👗 *admission charge.*

Dvořák Museum

Muzeum Antonína Dvořáka is well worth visiting. The museum inhabits a lovely Baroque villa originally called the Michna Summer Palace, built by Dientzenhofer in 1720. The charming façade is a delightful combination of ochre plasterwork and yellow stone. The museum displays scores and editions of the composer's works, and you can enjoy recordings of Dvořák's music as you wander through the building.
✉ *Ke Karlovu 20, (southeast of Charles Square), Nové Město,* ☎ *224 981 013,* 🖥 *www.nm.cz*
M *IP Pavlova, (tram: 4, 10, 16, 22, 23),* 🕐 *10:00–17:00 Tue–Sun,*
👗 *admission charge.*

The Prague Jewellery Cabinet

An amazing jewellery exhibition featuring decorative items from the 17th century to the present.
✉ *Hergetova cihelna, Cihelná 2, (near the Charles Bridge),* ☎ *221 451 400.*

Výstaviště

Beyond the National Gallery of Modern Art (*see page 37*) is the complex constructed originally for the 1891 **Prague Exhibition** and which is now a popular funfair and entertainment centre. The chief building is the **Industrial Palace**, an iron and glass structure with a vertiginous open-air spiral staircase to its clock tower. The Art-Nouveau **Lapidarium** (rebuilt in 1907) contains the National Gallery's collection of sculptures and is especially worth viewing. There is also a planetarium, a diorama, gardens through which to wander and the latest attraction, the **Seaworld** aquarium, www.morsky-svet.cz

Below: *The Michna Summer Palace, home of the Dvořák Museum.*

Stromovka Park

Contiguous with the Exhibition Grounds, Stromovka Park (more properly, the Royal Enclosure) was created in the 13th century and opened to the public in 1804. It is one of the city's largest green areas. Within the park is a lovely **Summer Palace** (*Mistodržitelský letohrádek*). This Neo-Gothic building dates from 1805 and until 1918 it was the official residence of the Governor of Bohemia. It now houses the National Museum's collection of newspapers and periodicals but is closed to the public. Elsewhere in the park there are various formal gardens and the remains of buildings long abandoned. The main path through the park crosses the Vltava, where there is a pleasant view from the bridge. By this point, the countryside begins to beckon and Prague city centre seems a long way off.

Below: *The beautiful Royal Garden.*

Parks and Gardens

Ledebour Garden

Ledeburská zahrada comprises a series of terraced gardens beneath Prague Castle. Gardens replaced vines here in the 16th century, and in the 18th century Baroque statuary and fountains were added. With staircases and balustrades, archways and loggias, the garden possesses a bewitching combination of faded formality and stunning views.
⊠ *Valdštejnská, Malá Strana,* ☺ *10:00–18:00 daily Apr–Oct,* 🛇 *admission charge.*

Royal Garden

The gardens were established in the 1530s by Ferdinand I and have since undergone many changes. The fountains, lawns and flower beds are immaculately maintained and you can enjoy superb views.
⊠ *second courtyard, Prague Castle,* ☺ *10:00–18:00 Apr–Oct,* 🛇 *free.*

South Gardens

On the south side of the castle, Josip Plečnik's staircase leads down from the third courtyard of the Royal Palace to the South Gardens (*Jižní zahrady*). Plečnik's two pavilions and basin in the **Paradise Garden** (*Rajská zahrada*) sit rather uneasily with the Baroque pavilion and statuary elsewhere in the gardens.
⊠ *Prague Castle,* ☺ *10:00–17:00 daily Apr–Oct.*

Botanical Gardens

These 19th-century *Botanická zahrada* are charming to wander through, especially in summer.
⊠ *Na slupí 16, Vyšehradská, Nové Město,* ☺ *10:00–17:00 daily,* 🛇 *free.*

SPORT AND RECREATION

ACTIVITIES
Sport and Recreation

A variety of sport and recreation facilities are available in Prague. **Ice skating** is the most popular winter activity and there are a number of public ice rinks in the city.

Tennis is also popular and the Czechs have produced world-class players such as Martina Navrátilová and Ivan Lendl. There are a few public tennis courts in the suburbs.

If you wish to **swim**, head down to one of the city's public swimming pools rather than brave the fairly polluted rivers.

Parks such as Letná Park, Petřín Hill and Stromovka Park are suitable for **walking** and **jogging**. There are also many fitness clubs and hotels with gyms.

Ice hockey and **football** are the two most popular spectator sports in Prague and it is possible to obtain tickets to these games (*see page 76*).

Alternative Prague

Prague has a fairly small gay and lesbian community which is mainly to be found around Vinohrady and Žižkov.

GayGuide.Net Prague (💻 www.gayguide. net/Europe/Czech/Prague) offers gay tourist information including accommodation, tours and services. Popular gay-friendly restaurants and cafés include **Érra Café** and **U Kapra**. The fashionable clubs and bars are the **A-Club** lesbian bar, and the popular and central **Friends Bar**. **Pinocchio** is not only a popular club – it also has a hotel, restaurant and café. *See page 77 for contact details.*

Ice Skating
Zimní Stadion
Štvanice
⊠ Štvanice ostrov, Holešovice
☎ 602 623 449,
💻 www.stvanice.cz
🕐 Sep–Mar
M Florenc

Tennis
Český Lawn Tennis
⊠ Štvanice ostrov 38, Holešovice
☎ 222 316 317
🕐 06:00–23:00, Apr–Oct
M Florenc

Swimming
Podolí Plavecký Stadion
⊠ Podolská 74, Prague 4
☎ 241 433 952
💻 www.pspodoli.cz
🕐 06:00–21:00 Mon–Fri, 08:00–19:45 Sat–Sun
M Tram 3, 16, 17, 21 to Kublov.

Below: *Ice hockey is a popular spectator sport in the Czech Republic. The national side has won the world championships on more than one occasion.*

41

Above: *A ride in a horse-drawn carriage is an enjoyable experience.*

Toy Museum
✉ Jiřská 6
☎ 224 372 294
🕑 09:30–17:30
💰 admission charge

National Technical Museum
✉ Kostelní 42
☎ 220 399 209
💻 www.ntm.cz
🕑 09:00–17:00 Tue–Fri, 10:00–18:00 Sat–Sun
🚌 45-minute tours at 11:00, 13:00, 15:00, Tue–Sun
💰 admission charge
🍴 café on premises

Prague Zoo
✉ U trojského zámku
☎ 296 112 111,
💻 www.zoopraha.cz
🕑 09:00–18:00 Apr, May, Sep, Oct, 09:00–19:00 Jun–Aug, 09:00–16:00 Nov–Mar
💰 admission charge
Ⓜ Nádraží Holešovice then bus 112

Fun for Children

There are many sights and activities in Prague that will amuse the younger generation. Museums such as the **Toy Museum** (*Muzeum hraček*), which is filled with dolls, model cars, trainsets and teddy bears, can be interesting while **Výstaviště**, Prague's Exhibition Grounds (*see panel, page 39*), contain an exciting funfair and entertainment centre.

Folk puppetry is a traditional art in the Czech Republic and is extremely popular. Street **puppet shows**, for which no knowledge of the Czech language is required, can be enjoyed by tourists of all ages. **Musicians** and **jugglers** are also popular street performers. Prague's **transport** can also be exciting. Children love the horse-drawn carts, trams, rowing boats and river cruises.

National Technical Museum

To the east of Letná, the National Technical Museum (*Národní technické muzeum*) has a large collection of scientific and industrial artefacts. Its history of transportation section in the main hall comprises an enormous range of bicycles, trains, motorcycles, cars and aeroplanes – there is even a hot-air balloon suspended from the rafters. The museum contains an interesting collection of astronomical instruments, and an exhibition devoted to clocks provides a cacophony of chimes on every hour. The basement – rather appropriately – has a large reconstruction of a coal mine (guided tours only).

Prague Zoo

Prague Zoo (*Zoologická zahrada*) adjoins the western border of Troja Park, on slopes which overlook the scenic Vltava – a chair-lift can be taken to the highest parts of the zoo grounds. All the usual inmates are present, but the most famous animals in the zoo are the diminutive Przewalski horses, part of the zoo's successful breeding programme. Young children usually love zoos, of course, so it's a good place for parents to bear in mind when youngsters are tired of looking at Baroque architecture.

Petřín Hill

Petřín Hill (*see page 46*) offers a variety of attractions for children such as the funicular railway, **Rozhledna** (a mini Eiffel Tower), a planetarium and an **observatory**. The crazily distorting mirrors of the **Mirror Maze** (*Zrcadlové bludiště*) provide amusement for visitors of all ages. The maze leads to a diorama depicting the defence of Prague against the Swedes on Charles Bridge in 1648.

Petřín Observatory
✉ Štefánikova hvězdárna, Petřín 205
☎ 257 320 540
🖥 www.observatory.cz
🕐 12:00–17:00, 19:00–21:00 Tue–Sun Mar–Oct; 14:00–19:00, 21:00–22:00 Tues–Fri, 10:00–12:00, 14:00–19:00, 21:00–23:00 Sat and Sun Apr–Aug; 13:00–18:00, 20:00–22:00 Tue–Sun Sep; 18:00–20:00 Tue–Fri, 10:00–12:00, 14:00–20:00 Sat and Sun Nov–Feb
M Tram 22, 23
🎟 admission charge

Rozhledna
✉ Petřín Hill
🕐 10:00–19:00 daily Apr–Oct, 10:00–17:00 Sat and Sun Nov–Mar
🎟 admission charge

The Mirror Maze
✉ Petřínské sady
☎ 257 315 212
🕐 09:30–18:30 daily Apr–Oct, 09:00–16:00 Sat and Sun Nov–Mar
🎟 admission charge

Below: *Prague Zoo is a popular attraction with young visitors.*

Below: *The 15th-century Powder Gate.*

Walking Tours
Walking Along Celetná

One of the oldest streets in Prague, Celetná (Map F–B2) gets its name from a kind of bread baked in the vicinity during the medieval period. The street heads east from Old Town Square, parallelling and intersecting with a warren of lanes and alleys. One exception to the Baroque uniformity of its shops and restaurants is the Museum of Fine Arts (*see* page 36).

The **Powder Gate** (*Prašná brána*) at the end of Celetná guards the entrance to Old Town (Map F–C2). A gate was first erected here in the 11th century: the present one – more a ceremonial tower than a defensive gate – dates from the late 15th century and was given its name after it was used to store gunpowder in the 17th century. Inside, there is a small exhibition on the history of the gate, and access to a viewing platform.

Old Town Square to Charles Bridge

North of Old Town Square, beyond the Old Town Hall, is the appropriately named **Small Square** (Map F–B3) (*Malé náměstí*). A prominent building here is the Rott House (*U Rotta*), a former ironmongery established in 1840 by V J Rott. Every available surface of this red house provides the basis for a complex series of paintings by the 19th-century Czech artist Mikuláš Aleš.

North of Small Square, Mariánské Square (Map F–A2) (*Mariánské náměstí*) is dominated by the **New Town Hall** (*Nová radnice*), built in 1911 on the east side of the square and designed by Osvald Polívka.

Further on are a number of Baroque buildings comprising the **Klementium** (*see* page 25). St **Saviour's Church** (*sv. Salvátor*) is part of the Klementinum complex and adjoins the entrance on **Knights of the Cross Square** (Map F–A3) (*Křižovnické náměstí*). Opposite St Saviour's is the **Church of St Francis** (see

page 34). In the centre of the square is the large bronze **statue of Charles IV** that was erected in 1848 to commemorate the 500th anniversary of the founding of the Carolinum (Charles University).

Above: *Medieval Charles Bridge, lined with Baroque statues.*

From the square, **Charles Bridge** awaits exploration, but allow some time to explore the waterfront to its left. Facing the river is a splendid Neo-Renaissance sgraffitoed building. Formerly the head office of Prague's water company, it now contains a riverside café, theatre and the first-floor **Smetana Museum** (*Muzeum Bedřicha Smetany*), from which there are good views of the river.

Southern Malá Strana

South of Lesser Quarter Square, between the river and the busy **Karmelitská** (Map B–E2), is **Maltese Square** (Map E–C1) (*Maltézské náměstí*). Ferdinand Brokof's statue of St John the Baptist is in the centre of the square, which is named after the Maltese Knights whose priory once stood here. Maltese crosses adorn the square, and the knights' church (Our Lady Beneath the Chain) can still be seen nearby.

Continuing from Maltese Square towards the river, cross over to **Kampa** (Map E–D2), the largest island in the river, separated

Tram 22

This is *the* tram for seeing the sights and for enjoying the best ride on the system. Starting off in the eastern suburbs, tram 22 wends its way through Míru and Charles Squares before turning left on Národní and crossing the river to the Lesser Quarter. A short straight leads to Lesser Quarter Square, after which there are the chicanes of Letenská. The tram then ascends to the castle via a series of hairpin bends and climbs still further to Strahov. An enormously long and fast straight takes it past Břevnov Monastery to its terminus at White Mountain.

Above: *Kampa Island sits alongside Charles Bridge and provides a peaceful refuge from the rest of the city.*

Kampa
Known as 'Little Venice' – solely because of the canal and former millrace called Devil's Stream (*Certovka*) which separates it from the left bank – Kampa was flooded repeatedly before the Vltava was dammed in the 1950s. The steps up to Charles Bridge were built to provide an exit from the island after many people drowned in one such flood. Before the fire of 1541 which swept through Malá Strana, Kampa's banks were also prone to instability, but flotsam created by the destruction of the blaze was used to strengthen the shifting shoreline.

from the Lesser Quarter by a canal and connected to Charles Bridge by flights of steps. There are three watermills on the island, plus a peaceful park and square in which to wander.

Petřín Hill
On the western flank of the Lesser Quarter, the steep, wooded slope of Petřín Hill (Map E–B2) climbs to a height of 318m (960ft), providing superb views over Prague. The largest green space in Prague, it is popular for walks and picnics.

You can either ascend the hill by following the winding paths or take the **funicular railway** (Map E–B2), which was originally built for the 1891 Prague Exhibition. Trains depart from the lower station near Ujezd. Disembark at Nebozízek station for a splendid view from the station restaurant.

At the top of the hill are the remains of Prague's **Hunger Wall** (Map E–B3) (*Hladová zed'*), which ascends the hill from the east and then follows a northwesterly direction toward Strahov Monastery. This was the southernmost part of Prague's old city walls, commissioned by Charles IV and completed in 1362. The story goes that Charles ordered it to be built in order to provide employment to the poor during a famine.

To the south of the summit station is the Observatory (*Hvezdárna*), and to the north is the Church of St Lawrence (*sv. Vavřinec*).

Beyond the church are more remnants of the exhibition, the most prominent of which is the 60m (200ft) **Observation Tower** (Map

E–A2) (*Rozhledna*). Based on the design of the Eiffel Tower, its top (reached by an interminable spiral staircase) provides panoramic views. Near the tower are the distorting mirrors of the **Mirror Maze** (*see* page 43).

Along the Vltava River

All roads heading west from Charles Square (Map F–B5) lead to the Vltava River, from where the islands of **Střelecký ostrov** and **Slovanský ostrov** (Zofín) (Map E–D3) can be reached. Both are pleasant places to stroll, but Zofín is the best – its attractive gardens are popular with walkers in summer and there are rowing boats for hire. Balls and concerts are held here throughout the year.

Rašínovo nábřeží (Map F–A5/6) – south along the river – is lined with rows of houses and mansions dating from the turn of the 20th century. Many are magnificent and ornately decorated but none are open to the public. Also on this road is possibly the most famous building constructed in Prague during the 1990s: the **Rašín Building** (*see* side panel).

Palacký Square (Map F–A6) (*Palackého náměstí*) lies to the south of the Rašín Building and is dedicated to the historian and politician **František Palacký**, one of the key figures in the Czech national revival of the 19th century. His Art-Nouveau monument in the middle of the square was designed by Stanislav Sucharda and depicts the world of imagination.

The Rašín Building
The Rašín Building (Map F–A6) on Rašínovo nábřeží is also known as **Fred and Ginger** because its flared glass-curtained tower looks like the swirling skirts of a female dancer as she clings to her partner. Designed by **Frank Gehry** and **Vlado Milunič** (Canadian and Czech, respectively) it is situated next to a turn-of-the-century apartment block designed by Václav Havel's grandfather; the president and his family lived in one of the apartments. Whatever one thinks of the postmodernist building – and both its appearance and prominent location have certainly earned it some controversy – it is heartening that Prague's traditional progressivism in architecture continues.

Below: *Prague's many bridges span the Vltava.*

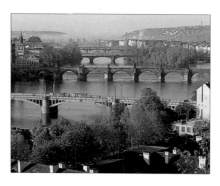

Organized Tours
UK: Czech Centre,
⊠ 13 Harley Street,
London W1G 9QG
☎ 020 7307 5180
✆ 020 7323 3709
Czech Tourist
Authority, ⊠ Suite
29–31, Morley House,
320 Regent Street,
London W1B 3BG
☎ 020 7631 0427
✆ 020 7631 0419
🖳 www.czech
tourism.com

Prague: American
Express, ⊠ Václavské
náměstí 56, ☎ 224 219
992, ✆ 222 111 131
Czech Tourism
⊠ Vinhoradská 46, PO
Box 32, 12041 Prahy 2
☎ (420) 221 580 111
✆ (420) 224 247 516
✆ info@czechtourism.cz
🖳 www.visitczechia.cz
Fischer ⊠ Provaznická
13, Prague 1
☎ 221 636 363
✆ 221 636 117
Prague Information
Service
⊠ Lucerna Passage,
Vodickova 36, Prague 1
☎ 420 12 4444
🖳 www.prague-info.cz
Premiant City Tour,
⊠ Na příkopě 23
☎ 606 6001 23
DC Service ⊠ Břehová
3, ☎ 224 816 346
✆ 222 325 420
🖳 www.dc-service.com
AVE Travel, ⊠ Pod
Bavířkou 6, ☎ 251 552
129, ✆ 251 556 005
🖳 www.avetravel.cz
✆ Ave@avetravel.cz
Prague Sightseeing
⊠ Klimentská 52
☎ 222 314 661, or ask
at your hotel reception.

West of Wenceslas Square (map F–C4)

Off the northwest end of Wenceslas Square, **Jungmann Square** (*Jungmannovo náměstí*) is named after the famous writer and scholar **Josef Jungmann** (1773–1847), whose statue is in the middle of the square. There are some interesting buildings here, the most prominent of which is the **Adria Palace** on the south side. If you look carefully, you may also find a 1912 Cubist street lamp on the eastern corner of the square, beyond which is the unfinished colossus of the **Church of Our Lady of the Snows** (*Kostel Panny Marie Sněžné*), built in 1397. The extravagant altar and the sheer scale of the interior are worth admiring. Next door is a small public park, which was formerly the herb garden of a Franciscan monastery.

Národní heads west from the square. There are some fine Art-Nouveau buildings along the street: watch out especially for number 7 (which spells 'Praha' with its top windows) and number 9. Opposite them is the **Church of St Ursula** (*sv. Voršila*), an early Baroque church built in 1678. The greatest landmark on Národní, The **National Theatre** (Map F–A4) (*see page 72*), is at the western end of the street.

Organized Tours

Although Prague is compact and well served by public transport, it might be a good idea to get your bearings by taking a city sight-seeing tour. There are several available, some of which combine coach and boat trips. Some tours are arranged by theme, for instance a walk-

ing tour around the city's Old Town treasures, or a bus tour of Prague's famous residences.

Organized trips are also available to many of the excursion destinations described on pages 78–83. Many of them will include guided multilingual commentary, lunch and/or (depending on the destination) free museum entrance, wine-tastings, a sampling of mineral spring waters, or a glass of Becherovka liqueur. Tours generally start from náměstí Republiky or Wenceslas Square.

If you prefer, you can organize your excursions before you leave for Prague by contacting the **Czech Tourist Centre**. Or try any of the local operators – prices are competitive so it's worth shopping around. In general cheaper tours are offered by **Prague Information Service**. The American Express and Thomas Cook offices both offer extensive travel services besides sightseeing tours in Prague and the Czech Republic.

Above: *Národní Street, a bustling thoroughfare, leads west from Wenceslas Square.*
Opposite: *An Art-Nouveau wrought-iron and stained-glass canopy at Municipal House.*

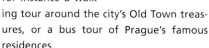

Cycling Tours
Specialist cycling tours through interesting and scenic areas of the Czech Republic are organized by MIKE, a travel agency based in Mělník. Itineraries vary in degree of difficulty and accommodation is arranged along the route. For information, contact **Czech Tourist Centre** or write to **MIKE**, ✉ Ostruhová 62, CZ-276 01 Mělník, Czech Republic
🖳 www.mike.mnet.cz

Above: *Golden Lane, within Prague Castle, and its picturesque row of houses – now souvenir shops – are mostly given over to the tourist trade.*

Glass, Crystal and Porcelain

Bohemian glassware and porcelain are of exceptionally high quality and are prized throughout the world. Designs range from traditional to contemporary, from chunky vases to exquisite slim-stemmed wine glasses. The best glass and china is produced by **Moser** works in Karlovy Vary and is on sale in the **Bohemia Moser** shop at Na příkopě 12, Prague 1. Shops will pack your purchases securely and can arrange transport to your home, at a price of course.

Shops

The range and quality of goods available in Prague shops has improved beyond recognition since the transition from the old, centralized economy under communist rule to a market-based economy. A growing number of leading Western multinationals have been making their presence felt while the country as a whole is now wholly familiar with a consumer-oriented culture. One consequence of this is that it has become increasingly difficult to pick up genuine bargains as prices rise to match Western levels, though there are bargains to be had, especially in glass, ceramics, CDs, books and wooden toys.

Most of the city's best shops are concentrated round the centre, especially round Old Town Square, Pařížská, on and around Celetná, and around Wenceslas Square. As many of these areas are pedestrianized, strolling around looking in shop windows can be a pleasurable activity, though you'll inevitably be contending with crowds of other like-minded window-shoppers. It's worth wandering into some of the passages off Wenceslas Square to window shop and admire the architecture; for example, Lucerna and Koruna palaces.

Glass, Crystal and Porcelain

Some interesting specialist glassware shops include:

Crystalex

⊠ *Malé náměstí 6, Prague 1,*

🖳 *www.crystalex.cz*

Cristallino
✉ Celetná 12,
Staré Město, Prague, 1
☎ 224 214 852
🖳 www.crystallino.cz

Erpet Bohemia Crystal
✉ Staroměstské náměstí 27, Prague 1,
☎ 224 229 755,
🖳 www.erpet.com

Exclusive
✉ Vodičkova 28,
Prague 1,
☎ 224 162 586.

Karlovarský Porcelan
✉ Pařížská 2, Prague 1,
☎ 224 811 023.

Moser
✉ Na příkopě 12,
(also at Malé náměstí 11),
☎ 224 211 293,
🖳 www.moser-glass.com

Musical instruments and CDs
Agharta
Great jazz-only music shop.
✉ Krakovská 5,
☎ 222 211 275,
🖳 www.arta.cz

Franz Kafka
✉ Kinský Palace (see page 35).

Philharmonia
Excellent classical music selection.
✉ Pařížská 13.

Praha Music Centers
✉ Revoluční 14.
✉ Soukenicka 20.

Týnská Galerie
Outstanding folk and classical selection.
✉ Staroměstské náměstí 14.

Bookstores
Even if you don't read Czech, it's a treat to browse round Prague's second-hand book-shops (antikvariát) as they are so attractively laid out, and there's often a good selection of old prints and posters. There are, however, also a number of English- and foreign-language bookstores, two of which – the Globe and U Knihomola (Bookworm) – also have cafés.

(see page 35).

The Vinohradský Pavilon
For indoor shopping, the **Vinohradský Pavilon** at Vinohradská 50 is an exclusive commercial centre. It occupies the site of a former fruit and veg-etable market. Over 60 brand-name boutiques selling everything from clothes, sportswear and household goods to electronic equipment are clustered under the Neo-Renaissance roof. Open seven days a week, 09:30–21:00 Monday to Saturday, 12:00–20:00 Sunday.

Music Stores
Musical instruments are beautifully made and less expensive than in the West. Sheet music is also cheaper. Classical music buffs will be impressed by both the range of CDs available and the advantageous prices. One of the best places to buy classical music is the **Franz Kafka Bookshop**; and **Bonton Land** in the Koruna Centre (near Můstek Metro) for all types of music. Other good music shops can be found all over the city, especially along Pařížská, Národní, Na příkopě and Jungmannovo (off Wenceslas Square).

Academia

English-language history and art books, with a café upstairs.
⊠ *Václavské náměstí 34 or Národní 7, Prague 1,*
☎ *224 223 511,*
🖳 *www.academia.cz*

Big Ben Bookshop

⊠ *Malá stupartská 5, Prague 1,*
☎ *224 826 525,*
🖳 *www.bigben bookshop.com*

Globe

⊠ *Pštrossova 6, Prague 1,*
☎ *224 934 203,*
🖳 *www. globebookstore.cz*

Knihkupeství U cerné Matky Boží

Bookstore in the house of the Black Madonna.
⊠ *Celetná 34,*

Prague 1,
☎ *224 211 275.*

U Knihomola International Bookstore

Generally a selection of classier coffee-table books and the like.
⊠ *Mánesova 79, Prague 2,*
☎ *222 729 348.*

Pod Kinskou

Specialist in paintings and antique furniture (closed Sunday).
⊠ *Náměstí Kinských 7, Prague 5,*
☎ *257 311 245,*
🖳 *www.antique-shop.cz*
Ⓜ *Můstek.*

Department Stores
Tesco

Everything from groceries to hi-fi equipment. Open 7 days.
⊠ *Národní třídal 26, Prague 1,*
☎ *222 003 111,*
🖳 *www.tesco_shop.cz*

Krone

Good grocery store. Open 7 days.
⊠ *Václavské náměstí*

Opposite: *Prague's traditional folk puppets are displayed on market stalls all around the city.*
Below: *The fruit and vegetable market on Havelská.*

21, Prague 1,
☎ 224 230 477,
🖳 www.odkrone.cz

Kotva

Large store with food
hall on lower floor
(see panel, page 52).
⊠ náměstí Republiky
8, Prague 1,
☎ 224 801 111,
🖳 www.od-kotva.cz

Baťa

Well respected
shoe store.
⊠ Václavské náměstí
6, Prague 1,
☎ 224 218 133.

Markets

Markets are good
places to browse
round and watch
some good-natured
haggling, though the
quality of the goods
on offer is not always
very high. The largest
and oldest market is
held at **Holešovice** in
converted abattoir
buildings at Bubenské
nábřeží 306.
Everything is here,
from fruit, vegetables
and poultry to elec-
tronic gadgets. In the
city centre, there is a

popular open-
air market in
Havelská that
specializes in
fruit, veg-
etables and
wooden toys.
Undoubtedly
the best time
for markets is in
the weeks run-
ning up to Christmas,
when Old Town
Square is taken over
by wooden stalls sell-
ing everything from
hot spiced wine to
candles, jewellery,
ceramics, puppets and
handmade crafts.
Charles Bridge is
covered in street stalls
throughout the year,
and in summer these
are supplemented by
others around Old
Town Square, the
Castle and Na příkopě.
Some are run by Czech
artisans finding an out-
let for their designer
jewellery, watercolours,
wooden toys and
unusual artefacts, but
many offer mass-pro-
duced 'Russian' army
memorabilia, cheap
watches or other tacky
tourist merchandise.

Traditional Crafts
Original one-off designs
by up and coming
young Czech artists
make fabulous and
surprisingly affordable
gifts. There are many
shops for gifts in wood,
ceramics, jewellery,
puppets, etcetera
in the little streets
between Old Town
Square and Charles
Bridge as well as in Old
Town Square itself.
For more traditional
Czech souvenirs, there
is a wide variety of
handcrafted items
available, including
wooden toys, beauti-
fully painted Easter
eggs, ceramics and
figurines in folk dress.
For a good selection of
folk art:
Ceska lidova-remesla,
⊠ Národní 36,
Prague 1
⊠ Melantrichova 17,
Prague 1
⊠ Husova 12,
Prague 1

Right: *The entrance to the Grand Hotel Evropa.*

Accommodation
Although accommodation has become much easier to find in Prague, it is advisable to book in advance if you're travelling during the high season (Easter until Sep) or over Christmas. Hotels are clean and most have been modernized to meet acceptable standards. Self-catering apartments or rooms in private homes offer a cheaper alternative to hotel accommodation. For more information in the UK contact:

Czech Travel Ltd
✉ Essex
☎ (01376) 56 05 92
📠 (01376) 56 05 93
In Prague:
AVE Travel Agency
✉ Prague International Airport
☎ 220 114 674
📠 224 223 463,
also at:
✉ Pod Barvížkou 16,
☎ 251 552 6129
📠 251 556 005,
🖥 www.avetravel.cz
🖰 Ave@avetravel.cz"
CKM
✉ Mánesova 77, Prague 2, Vinohrady
☎ 222 718 834
📠 222 726 370
🖥 www.ckm-praha.cz
🖰 ckmprg@login.cz
Pragotur
☎ 221 714 130
📠 221 714 127
🖥 www.pis.cz
🖰 pragotur@pis.cz

WHERE TO STAY

There is no shortage of places to stay in Prague, and finding something to suit your budget poses little problem. Since 1989, many new hotels have sprung up, mostly catering for the luxury or business markets, while older hotels have been refurbished or brought up to international standards with greater or lesser degrees of success. Prague's best hotels in the best central locations are inevitably the most expensive, and you'll need to make reservations before you travel. A number of new hotels with good facilities are situated in the suburbs, though their location is usually inconvenient for sightseeing. There are very few cheap or moderately priced hotels in the vicinity of Old Town, Prague Castle or the Lesser Quarter.

Hotels by no means offer the only accommodation option in Prague. Rooms in private homes or self-catering apartments offer sometimes significantly cheaper alternatives to hotels; a room in a family home is less impersonal and is an excellent way of making Czech friends.

Central Prague

• *LUXURY*

Grand Hotel Bohemia

(Map F–C2)

Large, luxurious hotel situated in the Old Town next to the Powder Gate. It has 78 air-conditioned rooms and suites, a 20th-century neo-Baroque Boccaccio Ballroom, a gourmet restaurant and parking is also available. Expensive.

✉ *Králodvorská 4,*
☎ *234 608 111,*
📠 *222 329 545,*
🖥 *www. grandhotelbohemia.cz*
🖱 *office@grandhotel bohemia.cz*
M *Náměstí Republiky.*

Paříž

(Map F–C2)

A glorious Art-Nouveau building that was declared a historic monument in 1984. Rooms are disappointingly bland compared to the beautiful craftsmanship on display in the hotel's public spaces, but they are comfort-able and well maintained. Live music and jazz concerts are regular features in the Café de Paris.

✉ *U Obecního domu 1, Prague 1,*
☎ *222 195 195,*
📠 *224 225 475,*
🖥 *www.hotel-pariz.cz*
🖱 *booking@ hotel-pariz.cz*
M *Náměstí Republiky/Můstek*

• *MID-RANGE*

Adria

(Map F–B4)

Good central location on Wenceslas Square, though bear in mind that this area turns into the city's disco and red-light district at night.

✉ *Václavské náměstí 26, Prague 1,*
☎ *221 08 21 11,*
📠 *221 08 13 00,*
🖥 *www.hoteladria.cz*
🖱 *accom@hoteladria.cz*

Atlantic

(Map F–C2)

Right in the heart of Prague, this hotel has 60 rooms, two restaurants and a winter garden.

✉ *Na Poříčí 9, Prague 1,*
☎ *224 811 084,*
📠 *224 812 378,*
🖥 *www. hotel-atlantic.cz*
🖱 *info@ hotel-atlantic.cz*
M *Můstek.*

Betlém Club

(Map F–A3)

On a quiet square in a 13th-century Gothic house. Small rooms but very central.

✉ *Betlémské náměstí 9, Prague 1,*
☎ *222 221 574/5,*
📠 *222 220 580,*
🖥 *www.betlemclub.cz*
🖱 *betlem.club@ login.cz*

Černý slon
(Black Elephant)

(Map F–B2)

An old 14th-century mansion situated next to Týn Church.

✉ *Týnská 1, Prague 1,*
☎ *222 321 521*
📠 *222 310 351*
🖥 *www.hotel cernyslon.cz*
🖱 *slon@hotel cernyslon.cz*
M *Staroměstská.*

Evropa

(Map F–B3)

Prague's legendary Art-Nouveau hotel in the centre of Wenceslas Square. The exterior façade and furnishings are stunning, the rooms less so.

✉ Václavské námestí 215, Prague 1,
☎ 224 228 215,
📠 224 224 544,
🖱 info@ evropahotel.cz
💻 www. evropahotel.cz
Ⓜ Mũstek.

U klenotnika

(The Jewellers)

(Map F–B3)

Eleven small, clean rooms close to Staroměstské náměstí and Václavské náměstí. A bargain.

✉ Rytířská 3, Prague 1,
☎ 224 211 699,
📠 224 221 025,
💻 www. uklenotnika.cz
🖱 info@uklenotnika.cz
Ⓜ Mũstek.

• BUDGET

Bílý Lev

(Map F–D2)

Clean, simple and comfortable.

✉ Cimburkova 20, Prague 3,
☎ 222 780 730,
📠 222 780 465,
Ⓜ Florenc.

Pension Unitas

(Map F–A3)

Former prison cells (President Havel was once a detainee) converted into two-, three- and four-bed accommodation for visitors on a shoestring.

✉ Bartolomějská 9,
☎ 224 211 802, 📠 224 217 555, 💻 www.uni tas.cz 🖱 unitas@uni tas.cz Ⓜ Národní třída

U krále Jiřího

(The King George)

(Map F–A3)

Charming little pension, with Prague's only Irish pub.

✉ Liliová 10, Prague 1, Staré Město,
☎ 224 248 797,
☎/📠 222 221 707,
💻 www.king george.cz
🖱 kinggeorge@ kinggeorge.cz
Ⓜ Staroměstská.

Hradčany

• LUXURY

Savoy

(Map B–A2)

A stylish hotel under the management of Vienna International Hotels and Restaurants. Superbly located just a few steps from Prague Castle. Every Sunday there's a jazz brunch in the hotel's acclaimed restaurant.

✉ Keplerova 6, Prague 1,
☎ 224 302 430,
📠 224 302 128,
💻 www.hotel-savoy.cz
🖱 info@hotel-savoy.cz
Ⓜ Malostranska

• MID-RANGE

U krále Karla

(The King Charles)

(Map B–B2)

A beautiful Baroque house situated within the castle distict at the top of Nerudova.

✉ Úvoz 4,
☎ 257 533 584,
📠 257 531 049,
💻 www. romantichotels.cz
🖱 ukralekarta@ romantichotels.cz
Ⓜ Malostranská.

U raka
(The Crayfish)
(Map B–A1)
This preserved 18th-century wooden house is situated in a quiet street. It has six double rooms.
✉ Černínská 10, Prague 1, Hradčany,
☎ 220 511 100,
☏ 233 358 041,
✿ info@romantik hotel-uraka.cz

Northern Prague
• *LUXURY*
Crowne Plaza
(Map D–A2)
A large towering building built in the time of Stalin, this hotel offers excellent facilities and charming service. Expensive.
✉ Koulova 15, Dejvice, Prague 6
☎ 296 537 263,
☏ 296 537 847,
🖳 www.crowne plaza.cz
✿ sales@crowne plaza.cz
M Dejvická, then tram 20, 25.

Holiday Inn Prague
(Map D–A1)

The former Hotel International (since completely transformed) offers four-star rooms away from the city centre.
✉ Na Pankráci 15/1684, Prague 4,
☎ 261 175 000,
☏ 261 175 001,
🖳 www.holidayinn.cz
✿ main@holidayinn.cz
M Vyšehrad

• *MID-RANGE*
Alta
(Map D–D2)
Beautiful hotel with 87 well-appointed rooms, a restaurant and other first-class facilities.
✉ Ortenovo náměstí 22, Prague 7,
☎ 220 407 011,
☏ 220 800 259,
🖳 www.hotelalta.com
✿ alta@login.cz
M Nádraží Holešovice.

Expo
(Map D–C2)
Large hotel with clean, comfortable rooms close to the exhibition grounds.
✉ Za Elektrárnou 3 Výstaviště, Prague 7,
☎ 266 712 470,
☏ 266 712 469,

🖳 www.expoprag.cz
✿ hotel@expoprag.cz
M Nádraží Holešovice.

Parkhotel Praha
(Map D–C2)
A large and somewhat impersonal hotel located on the road from the airport, 15 minutes from the city centre; conference facilities.
✉ Veletržní 20, Prague 7,
☎ 220 131 111,
☏ 224 316 180,
🖳 www. parkhotel-praha.cz
✿ hotel@ parkhotel-praha.cz

Vyšehrad
• *LUXURY*
Don Giovanni
(Map F–D3)
A new international 400-room hotel slightly out of the centre of Prague. Predominantly aimed at business visitors; facilities include restaurant, pub and café/bar, fitness club and conference rooms.
✉ Vinohradská 157a, Prague 3, Vinohrady,
☎ 267 031 502,

✆ 267 036 717,
🖳 info.prgdon@
dorint.com
🖳 www.dorint.
com/prag
M line A, Želivského.

• MID-RANGE
Luník
(Map: F–D6)
Modern hotel with
clean and simple
rooms.
✉ Londýnská 50,
Vinohrady,
☎ 224 253 974,
✆ 224 253 986,
🖳 hotel.lunik@
email.cz
M IP Pavlova.

• BUDGET
Pension City
(Map F–D6)
Located in a central,
but quiet area. Bright
and clean rooms.
✉ Belgická 10,
Prague 2, Vinohrady,
☎ / ✆ 222 521 606,
🖳 www.hotelcity.cz
🖳 hotel@hotelcity.cz
M Náměstí Míru.

Malá Strana
• LUXURY
Pod Věží
(Under the Tower)
(Map B–E3)

An extremely elegant
hotel well situated
beneath the Lesser
Quarter Bridge Tower
There's also a
restaurant that
specializes in Czech,
Jewish and inter-
national cuisine.
✉ Mostecká 2,
11800, Prague 1,
☎ 257 532 041,
✆ 257 532 069,
🖳 www.
podvezi.com
🖳 hotel@podvezi.com
M Malostranská.

**Residence
Nosticova**
(Map E–C1)
Historic house with 10
luxurious apartments,
furnished with
original artworks.
Each has a modern
kitchenette, bath-
room, colour satellite
TV and direct dial
telephone.
✉ Nosticova 1, 11800,
Prague 1,
☎ 257 312 513,
✆ 257 312 517,
🖳 www.
nosticova.com
🖳 info@
nosticova.com
M Malostranská.

U tři pštrosů
(The Three Ostriches)
(Map E–C1)
A charming
Renaissance town-
house adjacent to
Charles Bridge.
✉ Dražickeho
náměstí 12,
☎ 257 532 410,
✆ 257 533 217,
🖳 www.utripstrosu.cz
🖳 info@upstrosu.cz
M Malostranská.

• MID-RANGE
Dům U velké boty
(House at the
Big Shoe)
(Map E–B1)
Beautifully converted
townhouse in a
peaceful back street.
Only 12 rooms.
✉ Vlašská 30,
☎/✆ 257 533 234,
🖳 info@uvelkeboty.cz
🖳 www.dumu
velkeboty.cz
M Malostranská.

**Pension
Dientzenhofer**
(Map E–C2)
Extremely popular
and reasonably priced
pension. Birthplace
of Dientzenhofer,
Prague's greatest

Baroque architect.
⊠ Nosticova 2,
☎ 257 316 830,
📞 257 320 888
🖰 dientzenhofer@
volny.cz
Ⓜ Malostranská.

U modrého klíce
(The Blue Key)
(Map B–E2)
Friendly, well-run
hotel in a neatly
renovated palace.
The quieter rooms
are at the back.
⊠ Letenská 14,
☎ 257 534 361,
📞 257 534 372,
🖥 www.bluekey.cz
🖰 bluekey@
mbox.vol.cz
Ⓜ Malostranská.

• BUDGET
U Kříže (The Cross)
(Map E–C2)
Basic, modern hotel
in a Baroque building
on a busy street.
⊠ Újezd 20, Prague 1
☎ 257 313 272,
📞 257 312 542,
🖰 hotel@ukrize.com
Ⓜ Malostranská.

Hostels
Clown and Bard
(Map F–D3)

A cheap, cheerful
and clean hostel.
⊠ Bořivojova 102,
Žižkov,
☎ 222 716 453,
📞 222 719 026,
🖥 www.
clownandbard.com
🖰 clownandbard@
clownandbard.com
Ⓜ Jiřího z Poděbrad.

Kolej Jednota
(Map F–D3)
⊠ Opletalova 38,
Prague 1,
☎ 224 211 773 / 4,
🖰 kolej-jednota@
kam-cuni.cz
Ⓜ Hlavní nádraží.

Junior Hotel Praha
⊠ Senovážné 21,
Prague 1,
☎ 224 231 754,
📞 224 221 579,
🖰 euroagentur@
euroagentur.cz
🖥 www.
euroagentur.cz
Ⓜ Náměstí Republiky.

Pension Týn
(Map F–B2)
An excellent location
in the heart of the
Old Town.
⊠ International
Youth Hostel, Tynská

19, Prague 1,
☎ 602 642 159,
📞 224 808 233
🖰 backpacker@
razdva.cz 🖥 www.
hostel-tyn.web2001.cz
Ⓜ Náměstí Republiky.

Camp Sites
Intercamp Kotva Braník
(Off maps)
Camping, caravanning
and chalets on the
edge of the Vltava.
Cheap and quiet.
⊠ U Ledáren 55,
Braník, Prague 4,
☎ 244 461 712,
📞 244 466 110,
🖥 www.kotvacamp.cz
🖰 kotva@
kotvacamp.cz
🕘 Apr–Oct,
Ⓜ Karlovo náměstí
to Nádraží Braník,
then tram 3 or 17.

Camp Fremunt
(Off maps)
Tents, caravans and
bungalows in a quiet,
green environment
Trojská 159, Prague 7,
☎ / 📞 283 850 476
🖥 www.volny.cz/
campfremunt/
🖰 campfremunt@
email.cz

That Vegetarian Quest

As is usual in eastern Europe, non-meat eaters should expect a fair amount of pavement pounding in search of that elusive square meal. The situation in Prague has improved, but Czechs still find it difficult to comprehend that anyone should contemplate giving up meat. For this reason alone, beware the phrase *bez masa* ('without meat') on some menus: it often indicates merely that the main ingredient is not meat – there can still be (recognizable) animal matter in the dish. Czech cuisine is probably best avoided, but see page 63 for some vegetarian restaurants.

EATING OUT
What to Eat

Prague offers literally hundreds of affordable eating options, from cafés and pizzerias to bistros and Czech vinarnas. Visitors with deeper pockets will enjoy seeking out the city's better hotel restaurants and gourmet temples.

Breakfasts vary in size, from simple continental-style meals with bread, jam, tea or coffee, to slap-up hot and cold buffets at the larger hotels.

A traditional Czech **lunch** (*oběd*) or **dinner** (*večeře*) tends to be a straightforward, hearty affair, dominated by no-nonsense slabs of meat (*maso*) accompanied by simple dumplings, potatoes or rice and a sauce/gravy (sauces are uncomplicated and with no strong spices). Meals may commence with vegetable soups (*polévka*) or beef broths with liver dumplings, or appetizers like stuffed eggs, or ham stuffed with cream and horseradish (*plněná šunka*). Otherwise, starters can be little more than a range of cold meats. A selection of bread (*chléb*) accompanies most formal meals and when truly fresh is very good indeed.

Opposite: *Simple Czech cuisine: pork and dumplings.*
Right: *In summer, many cafés extend out onto the streets and squares.*

Fish and fowl are also favourites: something served everywhere is *Pečená kachna* – roast duck with bacon dumplings and sauerkraut. Carp and trout are the most significant fish in Czech cuisine, with carp being the traditional Christmas treat.

Vegetable accompaniments are often small, while salads are probably best avoided – ingredients are sometimes not very fresh, though this has become less of a problem than it once was.

The ubiquitous dumpling even puts in an appearance in some puddings: in *Ovocné knedlíky*, fruit dumplings (fruits surrounded by a sweet dough) are served with icing sugar and poppy seeds. Strudels are also very popular, as are pancakes (*palačinky*), stuffed with fruit, jam or ice cream.

Traditional Czech **snack foods** are *Chlebíčky* (open sandwiches on sliced baguettes), which can be bought from delicatessens and snack bars. They come with a range of fillings, often involving smoked fish and cream cheese. Sausages are popular, served either as hot dogs from street stalls or as *klobásy* (speciality sausages) from specialist shops. Street stalls also serve a *bramborák*, which is a potato pancake served on paper.

What to Drink

The Czechs' consumption of alcohol is among the highest in the world, and Czech **beers** (*pivo*) are justly famous. They are all excellent and some are very strong, so if you are new to them, be careful. Opt for draught beer if you have a choice.

Wining in Czech
Most visitors will be unfamiliar with the wines of the Czech Republic, none of which are exported overseas (often, it must be said, for good reason). Many of the whites are appallingly sweet even when they are described as dry, and it is safer to stick to reds. These include **Frankovka** and **Vavřinecké**, which are certainly worth drinking. Local sparkling wines (*sekt*) are cheap and drinkable in small doses. In August, the newly fermented Burčák becomes available. It tastes like grape juice and can be drunk as if it were, leaving ample time for a nauseous repentance.

Czech **wine** mostly comes from Moravia rather than Bohemia and much of it is reminiscent of German wine. There are some very good **fruit brandies** traditionally reserved for post-prandial drinks: *slivovice* (plum brandy) is the best known (and probably best left alone unless you have time to acquire the taste). *Becherovka* is a herb drink served as a liqueur or chilled as an apéritif.

Coffees are often poor affairs, while **tea** is taken weak and without milk, but the tea bag is served so you can play around with it.

Above: *Prague is famous for its pubs and beer halls.*
Opposite: *The U Kalicha pub benefits from its associations with* The Good Soldier Svejk.

Speaking Czech
Any attempt to speak the language will be appreciated. It is difficult to master, but here are a few guides as to the pronunciation. The stress should be on the first syllable.
c like **ts** in coa**ts**
ch like **ch** in lo**ch**
č like **ch** in **ch**urch
ě like **ye** in **ye**s
ň like **n** in **n**euter
ř like **rs** in Pe**rs**ian
š like **sh** in **sh**oot
ť like **ty** in no**t ye**t
ž like **s** in plea**s**ure

Where to Eat

It is possible to find somewhere to eat at almost any time of day, at least between the hours of 10:00 and 02:00. From simple stand-up fast-food stands (*bufet*) and cafés (*kavárna*) to upmarket wine cellars (*vinárna*) or restaurants (*restaurace*), the choice is much wider than you might expect. Traditional Czech food may be sampled in beer halls (*pivnice*), though the emphasis here is usually on downing litres of the local brew. There are a number of well-known hamburger chains for the inveterate fast-food addict.

The dearth of good, cheap hotels is more than outweighed by the number of excellent, reasonably priced eating establishments to be found all over Prague. The choice is varied, too, from cheap cafés and pizzerias to one of the most expensive French restaurants in the Czech Republic (*see* U Malířů, page 67). In between is a whole